VOLLEYBALL
Fastest Growing Sport
in the World!

HERE IS WISHING YOU ALL A
TERRIFIC VOLLEYBALL READING EXPERIENCE

Michael O'Hara

VOLLEYBALL

Fastest Growing Sport in the World!

The Basic Guide to the Sport Challenging Soccer

By Michael O'Hara

IP Publishing

Irish Pub Publishing
1239 El Hito Circle
Pacific Palisades CA 90272
310-454-4547

Library of Congress Cataloging-in-Publication Data

ISBN: 978-0-615-36414-8

Printed in the United States of America

Interior and Cover Design by Robert Aulicino

First Edition
10 9 8 7 6 5 4 3 2 1

*For my son, Ryan, who loves the sport of volleyball
just as much as I do.*
—MO'H

Table of Contents

CHAPTER 1———————————————————— 1
What the Sport of Volleyball Is All About
by Michael O'Hara

CHAPTER 2———————————————————— 21
Into Each Day Some Rain Must Fall by Michael O'Hara

CHAPTER 3———————————————————— 25
Olympic and Professional Volleyball by Dr. Doug Beal

CHAPTER 4———————————————————— 37
U.S. and International Beach Volleyball by Sinjin Smith

CHAPTER 5———————————————————— 45
The Magic of Four Women Volleyball by Gabrielle Reece

CHAPTER 6———————————————————— 51
Rules for Indoor and Beach Volleyball
by Dr. James Coleman

CHAPTER 7———————————————————— 57
Youth and High School Volleyball for Girls & Boys
by John Kessel

CHAPTER 8———————————————————— 69
Training Methods & Strategy Differences Between
Indoor and Beach Volleyball by Dr. Gary Sato

CHAPTER 9———————————————————— 73
Volleyball Clothing and Equipment by Michael O'Hara

CHAPTER 10——————————————————— 77
An Overview of Volleyball Injuries and Their Prevention
by Dr. Jonathan Reeser

CHAPTER 11 _____ 85
Why It Is Important to Get Every Member of the
Family Involved by Michael O'Hara

CHAPTER 12 _____ 89
Hollywood Moguls Develop the International Volleyball
Association by Michael O'Hara

CHAPTER 13 _____ 95
Team Cup Volleyball by Michael O'Hara

CHAPTER 14 _____ 99
FIVB International Women's Beach Volleyball
Championship-Hong Kong by Michael O'Hara

CHAPTER 15 _____ 103
The Contribution of Wallyball to the Sport of Volleyball
by Michael O'Hara

CHAPTER 16 _____ 109
Volleyball Guidelines for Parents, Referees,
Volunteers, and Fans by John Kessel

CHAPTER 17 _____ 125
The Opportunity to "Pay My Dues" as a Sports
Entrepreneur has Paid Off for the Sport of International
Volleyball by Michael O'Hara
Sports Illustrated December 11, 1972

CHAPTER 18 _____ 149
A Future Way That the International Sport of Volleyball
Could Become Even More Relevant

Author Biography by Michael O'Hara _____ 159

Author Acknowledgments by Michael O'Hara _____ 165

CHAPTER 1

What the Sport of Volleyball Is All About

by Michael O'Hara, Olympian

Your boss, the Athletic Director of the International YMCA's Training School, now called Springfield College, asks you to create a sport that can be played indoor, out of the winter weather. Dr. James Naismith jumps at the challenge, and comes up with thirteen basic rules for the game, and asks a school janitor to nail two wooden boxes to the gymnasium balcony to be used as goals. But the janitor can only come up with some half-bushel baskets. Voila! The sport becomes known as basketball. Each time a basket was scored, a ladder had to be brought onto the court to recover the ball. Obviously, that rule got changed, as did the preventing of dribbling the ball.

Many sports enthusiasts already know that story, of course. How America gave the world an entirely new sport that would go on to gain incredible popularity, generate billions of dollars in revenue, and in many ways change the world!

But there's another part of the story. A part that most people don't know.

Four years later, in 1895, a graduate of that same YMCA College, Dr William G. Morgan, in charge of the Holyoke, Massachusetts. YMCA learned from Naismith that basketball was considered too strenuous for many of their older male clientele, and he decided to come up with a better answer. Morgan turns out to also be a very clever man. The sport he invents is . . . Mintonette? Okay—Morgan wasn't such a great

1

namer. His sport was inspired by badminton, but it got rid of some of the equipment—namely the rackets.

Morgan simply took the rubber bladder out of the basketball, and elevated a badminton net to eight feet, and used a larger court. Fortunately for the world, Morgan's new game was renamed a few years later by Alfred Halstead—and WOW! a totally awesome and ideally suited sport was born—VOLLEYBALL!

Another gift to the world...for which we can all thank the YMCA.

Of course, as both sports have developed far beyond what Naismith or Morgan could ever have imagined, it's clear that the world class version of volleyball is potentially just as strenuous as basketball, with spikes clocked at smoking 100 mph speeds!

The spike itself, by the way, was added several years later to volleyball by the Filipinos, as the sport grew more popular internationally. The most significant recent rule change, however, was contributed by . . . me. It's called the "Rally Scoring System." We'll talk about it in detail in the chapter about the sport of Wallyball.

It wasn't all that long after its creation that volleyball started traveling the world with American missionaries. They were looking for common ground that could transcend the need for speaking the same language and that encouraged team togetherness. It was also very easy and INEXPENSIVE to set up a volleyball court. Many games were played in the desert, forest, or near water, using court lines being drawn in the sand, playing over fishing nets, vines, etc. depending upon the setting.

The other group that originally helped spread the sport worldwide was the American military. They used volleyball to keep their personnel fit and competitive. It was also an excellent way to attract non-service personnel and "locals."

It is often noted that sixteen thousand volleyballs were distributed to United States troops and Allied Forces in 1915, which became excellent tools for staying fit and getting to know the neighbors, wherever they traveled.

By 1953, when I first became seriously interested in the

sport, volleyball was already something of an international phenomenon.

I spent several years, as a preteen, playing "mano a mano" over a clothesline and using a thick large balloon for a ball! The fact that volleyball was great exercise and competitive fun was a huge bonus.

These two American sports, basketball and volleyball have become two of the three most played and watched sports in the world, with soccer, originated in Europe and South America, being the third and the oldest of the three. R.C. Cubbon, Physical Director at the Providence, RI YMCA (and a 1909 Springfield College student) in the 1917 edition of the Official Volleyball Rulebook wrote: "It is a recognized fact that baseball is the national game at the present time, but during the past two decades certain restrictions have been growing about this great game which are bound sooner or later to relegate it to a certain more limited group. I refer to the rapid development of congested city life, which has increased property values to the extent that city land for baseball is held at prohibitive prices. Baseball today has surrendered to the suburban towns, the rural districts, our educated institutions and professionalism. Baseball requires 4000 square feet and football 1500 square feet per player. These conditions will sooner or later jeopardize the popularity of the game. If this is true and we are becoming a game-loving people, and since we need games for our health's sake, we must look for additional sports."

In the early '60's the Japanese had the opportunity to host the Olympic Games in Tokyo, and therefore had the persuasive clout to include Indoor Volleyball in their Games. They had adopted the sport with great enthusiasm, both young and old, and had world class teams in both the men's and woman's divisions. The result was a Gold medal for the Japanese women's team and a Bronze medal for the men, which was the tallest team in the Olympic competition! Prior to those Olympics they made available to other television networks around the world a thirty minute tape showing a very frenetic coach, called

Diametsu, drilling his team harder than any other coach has ever drilled any other sport team! That showed the world that this was not a game for sissies, and when they won the Gold, most of the volleyball coaches worldwide started emulating his coaching style to some degree.

As a result of that tremendous achievement, over 80% of all of the monies flowing to the Federation Internationale de Volleyball (FIVB) to nourish the sport of volleyball throughout the world, from both television and sponsorship, has consistently come from Japan ever since.

One basic way to measure the size and strength of an amateur sports organization is by listing the number of National Federations a sport has throughout the world. In this country we call them National Governing Bodies [NGB's]. The third largest number, of all the Olympic Sports, is Soccer Football with 204 NGB's, and the second largest with 216 NGB's is Basketball. Also, volleyball's newest version of the sport, Beach Volleyball, has grown far faster in size and scope than its counterpart, Beach Soccer, which is also a fine and healthy sport. Soccer Football also enjoys a fabulous World Cup event, which places second in size and character only to the Olympic Games themselves. Both sports are exceptionally classy, and ideally suited for play by young boys and girls, and offer a far less injury prone approach than most other sports.

If we were to deal solely with playing population for all sports only, cricket would be included with soccer and volleyball. However, over ninety percent of the cricket players reside in India and Pakistan, and their growth pattern reportedly lags behind both soccer and volleyball. It is currently not an Olympic sport, and is not a National Governing Body in the USA and many other countries. Cricket is also not one of the Pan American Games sports for South, Central and North American countries.

Volleyball is one of the very few sports with two full-fledged Olympic disciplines, Beach and Indoor Volleyball, for a variety of reasons:

1. It is a very economical sport.
2. It is flexible—a fishing net or rope placed between two trees works!
3. It can be played on many different surfaces—hardwood, sand, grass, snow, artificial surfaces placed in convention centers, and even in water!
4. Any number on each side of the net may play. There is a terrific game played by three teams on three center connected nets. A sport called Big O's Santenis, which uses many of the same principles as volleyball, including the net and court, has just arrived on the scene.
5. It is an excellent co-educational activity, where boys and girls add the social element of being able to play well on the same team.
6. The net separates the teams, making it especially classy for women to play.
7. Eye catching action has made it a fine spectator sport.
8. It is a wonderful sport for television. Whether it is the lifestyle look of the beach or the indoor game, because the size of the court fits naturally into the camera lens, and the larger ball size is far easier to capture on camera than golf, tennis, or even baseball. Also, television techniques such as stop action, slow motion, and instant replay work extremely well.
9. It is very easy for the new sports fan or participant to understand the basic rules of the sport.
10. It requires a very small and inexpensive amount of equipment.
11. The sport of volleyball can be enjoyed by all ages, and they can play well on the court at the same time.
12. It is a sensational recreational activity, starting with club or school intramural programs, and fraternity and sorority leagues, working later in life with business and community leagues.

Due to these attractive features, the popularity of Volleyball has flourished all over the world, especially in all of the socialist countries, and in Asia. Japan initially changed the rules to

"Dad" Center—Outrigger Canoe Club VB Organizer brought VB to OCC

Duke Kahanamoku volleyball player

allow for their shorter stature. Their rules called for nine players per team, with four hitters and a setter permanently placed in the front row, and four more defensive only players positioned permanently in the back row. While the Olympic Movement caused them to return to the mainstream in 1964, there still remain many "mamason" leagues for housewives throughout Japan utilizing the nine women on a side configuration.

The migration of this unique sport to all nations began with the American missionaries. They were seeking a common ground that could transcend the need for speaking the same language and that encouraged team togetherness. The fact that Volleyball was great exercise and competitive fun was a huge bonus.

While the Russians and Cubans dominated the sport in the '60's and '70's, the American men's team captured the Gold medal in the '84 Los Angeles and '88 Seoul Games, captained by the World's Greatest Player of the Century—Karch Kiraly.

The greatest shot in the arm for the sport of volleyball, in my opinion, came from the magical source called the Olympic Games, both in the short and the long term. The Japanese were slated to host the Olympics in Tokyo, but along came World War II, so in came the cancellation by the International Olympic Committee IOC) of any Games, any place! That negative became a positive, however, both for Japan, and for the sport of Volleyball!

When the Olympics resumed in the late forties in London, the Japanese got back in line for hosting duties. By the time they were awarded the Games again, selected in 1958, for the 1964 Games, they were in a far better position to request permission from the IOC to allow volleyball to be added to their Tokyo hosting agenda. That was also excellent timing for me to be selected to play in this initial competition, representing the USA, whereas the original plan was far too early for me to participate.

It also gave our major volleyball leader, Dr. Harold Friermood, the national director of health and physical education for the National Board of the YMCA from 1943 to 1968, who also had served as President of the United States Volleyball Association from 1952 to 1955 and Vice President of the Federation Internationale de Volleyball (FIVB) from 1951 to 1960, the time to assist the Japanese to secure the votes for volleyball to be included in 1964.

Meanwhile, the Japanese found two of the most effective volleyball coaches in the world to develop teams that could medal at the '64 Tokyo Olympic Games. The women's coach that they hired, was Hirofumi Daimatsu, who came to be known as the demon coach, for his demanding and exhausting drills and strict discipline. His approach was so unique that a 30 minute television program was made, showing the hard spikes directly into the body, and the superb athletes crying loudly, but refusing to drop out of the drills. Just prior of their Olympics, it was filmed and shown around the world, and immediately destroyed the concept of volleyball being a dainty little sport for middle aged YMCA athletes. When the Japanese team reigned supreme, and won the Gold Medal (as I recall it was the only Gold Medal that Japan won that year).

The men's coach, Yatutaka Matsudaira, was hired, and he later became a close friend of mine, as we were attending annual meetings in Lausanne, Switzerland, and he sometimes needed me to help his assistant translate his report into English, which along with French were the only two official Olympic languages. He was tremendously creative and equally resourceful. His athletes were not only the tallest team in the tournament, but they also had fantastic quickness, along with the ability leap quickly, and dive on the floor to keep every ball coming to their side of the net controlled and returned quickly and deceptively.

While a lot less was expected of the men's team, they were captured the Bronze medal, and went on to win the Silver Medal in the Mexico 1968 Olympics, and the Gold Medal in the 1972 Munich Games! Many of the other countries that entered the volleyball Olympic competitions began to borrow many of the techniques that made both the female and male Japanese teams so successful.

This island community of Japan, with few natural resources, were on the way to becoming one of the most productive countries in the world because of their extremely intelligent and determined people, and dealing with the subject of volleyball was no exception.

There was a debate many moons ago, between the Outrigger Canoe Club (OCC) of Honolulu and the Santa Monica Beach Club (SMBC), as to where Beach Volleyball was conceived. My intensive research finally determined that the OCC, in 1916, invented Beach Volleyball, and began playing the six man, and later four man versions.

In 1929, SMBC hired the famous Hawaiian Olympic swimmer, Duke Kahanamoku, as their Director of Sports, and he brought Beach Volleyball along with him. That first winter one cold Monday morning, there were only four men ready to play Beach Volleyball. They thought about how they could still get a

OCC Beach VB Players Johnny Weismuller & Duke Kahanamoku

workout, and finally decided to draw a line down the center of the volleyball court, and played two on each side.

They enjoyed the extra exercise, so a few weeks later they agreed to try playing two man, while covering the entire court, and VOILA, Beach Doubles Volleyball was born!

Tom Haine OCC President 1968 VB Olympian

Tom Selleck Actor OCC VB player

Johnny Weismuller at Santa Monica Beach Club

Buster Crabbe, Actor Olympic swimmer, VB player, SMBC.

Pablo Johnson SMBC Beach VB innovator

A group of Outrigger members pose for a photograph on the volleyball court. Duke Kahanamoku is on the far right. c. 1915

Volleyball was an instant hit at the Outrigger with men, women and children participating.

Volleyball courts were centrally located and the game was popular with men and women of all ages.

Outrigger doubles champions.
From left: Bill Cross, Pat Wayman, Dr. Jim Beardmore, Pat O'Conner.

Doubles partners Pat Wayman and Tom Haine.

The Beach Club of Santa Monica, where beach doubles were initally played.

The American women's team captured the Silver medal, losing a hotly contested final match to a sensational team from China. In 1992, the American men and women's teams won the Bronze.

As eastern and western European teams began to dominate in the '90's, no medals were won by U.S. men and women indoor teams in the '96 Barcelona and 2000 Sydney Olympic Games. However, a ninth seeded American beach doubles team, Dane Blanton and Eric Fonoimoina, won the Gold medal in Sydney. In the Athens 2004 Games, our best USA Women's Beach Volleyball Team of Misty May-Treanor and Kerri Walsh captured the Olympic Gold medal in Athens, 2004, and defended their title in the 2008 Games.

The NCAA has just announced that they are expanding their Women's Volleyball Program to the beach! All of their Division II colleges and universities may start in the spring of 2011, and Division I may begin competing in 2012. Colleges and universities that currently have indoor programs will be motivated to bring in volleyball players that have developed their all around skills playing doubles in the summer on the beach. Since the two sports will be scheduled at different times, those same players will then be able to nourish the indoor teams of that college or university as well. Also, when gifted high school athletes try to decide whether to concentrate on basketball or volleyball, that require many of the same skills, they may favor the sport that will allow an athlete to play professional volleyball worldwide, either indoors or on the beach. It will also give them two chances to play in the Olympic Games, since both sports are individually presented in the Games, and sell out their event tickets, in the top 30% of all the Olympic sports!

The fact that our women's teams won the Gold medal in Beach Volleyball, and the Silver in Indoor Volleyball, in the 2008 Beijing Olympics becomes another motivator. The Men's Team did even better, earning the Gold medal in both Indoor and Beach Volleyball!

The following chart shows the consistent and tremendous growth they have achieved.

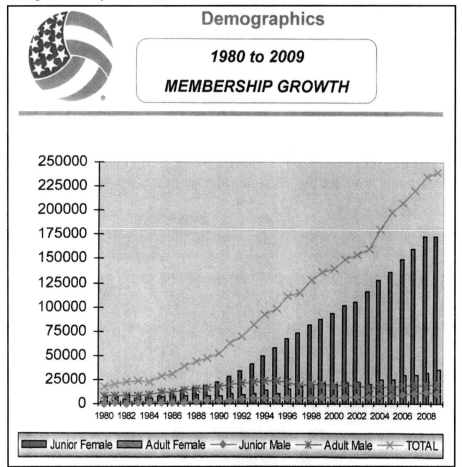

WHEN THE FEDERATION INTERNATIONALE DE VOLLEY-BALL (FIVB) STARTED THEIR GROWTH EXPANSION IN 1974, THERE WERE ONLY THIRTEEN CHARTER MEMBER NATIONS AS NATIONAL GOVERNING BODIES (NGB'S). THAT NGB GROUP IS CURRENTLY 220 NATIONS, AND GROWING! (NOTE: THE BASKETBALL AMERICAN NGB HAS RECENTLY REPORTED TO ME THAT THEIR SPORT HAS 216 NGB'S WORLDWIDE, AND THE SOCCER NGB REPORTED 204.)

CHAPTER 2

Into Each Day Some Rain Must Fall

by Michael O'Hara

The USAV has been doing well financially, despite the recession, due mainly to the tremendous, consistent growth of their membership. Like all other NGB's, they have never been nourished in any way by the Federal Government. They received a much appreciated contribution from the Los Angeles Olympic Organizing Committee, due to the financial success of the 1984 Olympics. Although the '32 Games in L.A. were slightly above the breakeven point, for the first time in Olympic history Los Angeles spent approximately $500 million and sold Games tickets, television rights, and sponsorship monies to realize almost $750 million!

Therefore, in early 1955, each of the twenty six NGB's participating in those Games received $1.3 million to invest in the administration of their sport. All of the NGB's were able to invest that windfall capital, and use financial return to nourish their many member groups, which, for the USAV, is currently about forty different publics i.e., the Youth, Seniors, Deaf, Sitting, Wheelchair, Open, etc.

However, it is not a perfect world, and one of the sports under their umbrella is Beach Volleyball. Karch Kiraly, named World's Best Player by the Federation International de Volleyball (FIVB) approximately a decade ago, has organized a fine series of tournaments for all male and female beach volleyballers throughout the United States and the program is going extremely well.

However, there is another series of volleyball tournaments

that is for the best players in the United States and the rest of the world that offers lots more prize money than Karch does. It is called the Association of Volleyball Professionals (AVP) and it has been operating since 1973, with a constant changing of leadership. Their profit centers have been predominantly sponsorship and ticket sales. While they operate under the auspices of USAV, a good part of the time they have been independent, and in some cases, territorial. On a few occasions, they have quietly produced tournaments in Mexico, and tried to do the same in Japan, until the FIVB learned of their transgression and came crashing down on their plans.

When the recession in America hit, many of the sponsors, including the AVP title sponsor, Crocs, suffered severe financial difficulty and pulled out, bankrupting the AVP, as of August, 2010. The idea of a shoe manufacturer being the title sponsor for a sport that is one of the few in the world that doesn't use shoes for their competitions, can now be questioned.

(left to right) 1968 Olympian Butch May and 1992 Hall of Famer Gene Selznick vs. Ryan and Michael O'Hara exibition match, won by the O'Hara's, played just before the 1986 Manhattan Beach Championship finals.

The USAV has just agreed to produce five new Beach Volleyball tournaments next summer, including the "Wimbledon of Beach Volleyball" the Manhattan Beach tournament. The co-producers of that tournament will be the city of Manhattan Beach (who are recognized around the sports world as hosting the finest beach volleyball tournament in the world), and the International Management Group, the finest sports sponsorship marketers inthe world, They would welcome an association with other individuals or business entities who would like to produce additional tournaments. The USAV will probably have the support and assistance from their most famous player and currently Assistant Coach of the USAV Woman's Indoor Volleyball Team, Karch Kiraly. This should be a strong step forward for this recovery program, and will produce, without question, more long range synergism than USAV enjoyed with the more independent AVP.

Meanwhile, the FIVB international Beach Volleyball circuit has moved more television coverage of excellent competition into the USA marketplace, keeping the sport moving forward in the eyes of the public.

Meanwhile, even with the recession affecting most cities worldwide, Beach Volleyball Tournaments continue to thrive in most parts of the world. The oldest professional tournaments started to be enjoyed in Italy over six decades ago. Japan saw volleyball start to challenge baseball in popularity, while Brazil now enjoys Beach and Indoor Volleyball almost as much as Soccer! In Poland, volleyball has become their number one sport.

One of the many important reasons for this growth pattern is that the six person volleyball, placing twelve athletes on the court, offers a greater density of players per square foot of real estate than any other sport! However, it doesn't appear crowded due to the specialization of each male or female athlete. Also, the net separates the combatants, allowing for the delivering of power spikes, and graceful digs, without injuring any of the twelve players. This is one of the only sports that delivers that highly desirable condition. It also allows the collaboration of players of different size, age and skill level to be on the team and deliver "specialized" contributions.

CHAPTER 3

Olympic and Professional Volleyball

by Doug Beal, USA Volleyball CEO

The high points or most significant events of men's international volleyball history are best described in the following eras: (1) the Japanese from 1964-72; (2) the Polish dominance because they won a world championship plus an Olympic Games and they brought a unique style of play; (3) the Soviet team between 1977-82; (4) the U.S. team from 1983-89; (5) the Italian team from 1990-2000, (6) Brazil from 2000-2007, and the US and Brazil since 2007.

The most significant event that took place in the history of volleyball, after the invention of volleyball, was its inclusion of male and female Indoor Volleyball in the Olympic Games in 1964 in Tokyo, Japan. Volleyball became an accepted worldwide team sport at that time. It was show-cased in the most significant sporting event in the world and has grown to have a very significant position in the Olympic Games. It has only been enhanced by the inclusion of two-person Beach Volleyball as a separate full fledged discipline starting with the 1996 Olympics in Atlanta. The inclusion of volleyball in the Olympic Games was accomplished in large measure in the1940's and 1950's by the work of some very significant American pioneers including Harold Friermood, along with Avery Brundage, who was President of the IOC (International Olympic Committee). Brundage was a staunch supporter of pure amateurism and fought very hard against the opening of the Olympics, in any form, to any athlete who was taking money.

The big controversy during his tenure was that it was a double standard being implicitly understood by most of the

Olympians: one for the western countries, and one for the eastern countries. At that time the Soviet Union, East Germany, and all of the eastern block countries essentially had no professional athletes. Every athlete was being state supported (many times as a member of the Armed Services) or paid to play on their national teams. In the western countries, there was this sort of amateur sporting development, as well as the professional sporting development. I think all of that changed with two events. One event was the fall of the Berlin Wall, which was the fall of Communism, and the fall of the social economic system in the mid to late '80's. The second event was the very gradual evolution in the thinking of the International Olympic Committee to open the Olympics to the world's best players with each Olympic Sport Federation deciding whether to allow professional players to participate.

That evolution started with the 1976, 1980, and 1984 Olympics and has only increased in amplitude in terms of more and more sport becoming self regulatory in the sense that there is essentially no difference between pro and amateur at the Olympic level. It now is simply eligible versus non-eligible, and basically if your sports international governing body says your're eligible, your're eligible. So the standards are very different but, as baseball has been removed from the Olympics, as volleyball has expanded, as basketball has had the NBA Dream Team, as soccer has allowed professionals, as track athletes have gotten huge money for appearances, and as tennis players have had professionals, there is essentially no difference anymore between the professional and the amateur athlete as far as the Olympic Games are concerned. I think in a very short period of time, any professional who wants to participate in any sport that happens to be included in the Olympic calendar will have the opportunity based solely on performance. The Olympics will truly be the highest level of performance of any event in the world.

Relative to Indoor Volleyball, there have been some remarkable performances in Olympic history, both on the men's side as well as the women's side. If we start with the men, in 1964 the Soviet Union dominated and won the first Olympic tournament. They repeated their triumph in 1968 in Mexico City. Although, an interesting sidelight of the 1968 triumph was that their only loss was in the opening match of the tournament to a significant underdog USA team. This was one of the highlights of the United States' performance in international volleyball until the 1984 Olympic. The Soviet Union won the first two Olympic Gold medals. They dominated the sport in the early '60's up to about 1970.

At this same time, the Japanese were evolving very quickly on the men's side under the leadership of Yasutaka Matsudaira, who in 1998, became the first Japanese to be inducted into the Volleyball Hall of Fame and in 2001 was chosen as Best Volleyball Coach of the 20th Century (Male) by the International Volleyball Federation. He was the coach of the Japanese team not too long before the 1964 Olympics. The only volleyball that was really popular in Japan was nine-person volleyball. So he led a very organized effort to develop six-man volleyball in Japan and the team got good enough that by the Tokyo Olympics, they were able to win a Bronze medal. In 1968 in Mexico City, they improved enough to be the Silver medalist. In 1972, still under the same coach, they won the Gold medal in Munich. I think they are the only team that has shown that very steady progress in the history of international volleyball: from a third place to a second place to a first place. Unfortunately for the future of Japanese volleyball, that is clearly the high watermark for men's volleyball in Japan thus far. They have never seriously since that time challenged for the Gold medal, although they did finish fourth in the 1976 tournament for men in Montreal. So certainly, one of the most renowned teams in Olympic history was this Japanese men's team that peaked in Munich in 1972 under coach Matsudaira.

The Japanese developed a style of play that popularized a lot of the techniques and a lot of the systems and tactics that are well integrated into the game today. Some such techniques are: combination plays, where one player moves around another player to spike the ball; quick attacks that almost all the teams are using today; safe effective techniques such as diving and rolling in the back court to save balls; and their training method was also something that became very popular world-wide for many years. This is also common: When someone wins an important event, everybody tends to copy the way they play. They used a lot of gymnastics tactics, individual coach with one player drills, individual hitting drills, individual digging drills, individual ball handling drills. This was common in Japan, and in the far east,— the almost spiritual ability of a male or female player to push themselves beyond their physical limit and work harder than they think they can work and accomplish things that they didn't think they could do!

Just before the 1972 Olympic Games, there was a little blip on the radar screen for men's volleyball. The East German team in 1970 won the World Championships and probably was the favored team going into Munich. The Olympics Games were in Germany, even though it was a divided Germany at the time. So, the Japanese victory in Munich was probably a little bit of an upset, although they beat this East German team in the finals in a fairly one-sided victory. Their closest was actually in the semi-finals when they earned a very close win against a very strong team from Bulgaria.

So as we progress through the men's volleyball history, the next Olympic Games were in 1976 in Montreal. For about a three year period from 1974-1976, the dominant men's team was a wonderful collection of players from Poland, under also a very famous coach, Hubert Whener. They won the World Championships in 1974, as well as the Olympic Games in 1976. I suspect that this team was the oldest team to ever win an Olympic gold medal. They were led by some Hall of Fame players. One of their middle blockers was Edward Skorek. It looked like a collection of middle aged gentleman out there playing, but they were a tremendous team. In 1974 at the World Championships, they played with two setters.

They may have been the last great men's team to win a world tournament, of any kind, with a two-setter system. After that tournament, one of the setters, Stan Gosciniak, retired and came to the United States to participate in a new professional league that had started. So, what they did was instead of trying to find another setter to plug into that system, they simply changed systems and put another hitter in and went to a 5-1 and won the Olympic Games in Montreal with a 5-1 system built around the setter that everybody had thought was not nearly as talented as Gosciniak, but they won. At the Olympic tournament in Montreal, it was a tournament that was in two pools, they played five sets in their pool play against everyone. They won in five sets against everyone, except one team in their pool. They were close to losing several times and had match point against them in the round-robin against Cuba. They won in five against Czechoslovakia. They won in five against Korea. It was a remarkable performance because several times it appeared as though the match was lost and some how they just sort of hung on and right at the end they won! They also won in five in the semi-finals against Japan and won in five in the finals against the Russians (Soviet Union at that time)! The Soviet Union team was very heavily favored.

A couple of other outstanding traits about Poland's team is that this team pretty much ran one offensive play in every rotation. They basically ran an "X" or a "reverse X," or what we call a "fake X," in every rotation. When the volleyball was passed to the setter, the hitter would run straight at him, and then slide to one side or the other to hit the spike. Everybody in the world knew exactly what Poland was going to do. However, they were so good at it, so precise, such good ball handlers, and had played together for so long that nobody could stop them. The only other new additional element that they brought in was that they initiated some back row hitting. They had one young player on their team that turned out to be perhaps one of the best players of all time, Thomaz Wojtowicz. He was the middle blocker that played opposite Skorek, and he hit out of the back row and when the match was on the line against the Soviet Union in the final gold metal match, they set every ball to him (note: this is the first time anybody probably, had ever seen this) when he was in every front row and back row position about two times around and he killed every ball he swung at! It was really one of the remarkable performances in the history of men's volleyball. They won the Gold medal! The score (using the now obsolete sideout scoring,) was 18-16 in the fifth set against a very heavily favored Soviet Union team. Unfortunately for the Poles, that is perhaps the last time they were really at the top of the world. A lot of the players continued, but a couple of them retired.

From 1977 until 1982, the Soviet Union won every major world event that was contested starting in 1977 with the World Cup; the 1978 World Championships; the 1980 Olympic Games, even though it was a boycotted games, they won in Moscow; the 1981 World Cup again; the 1982 World Championships again; and of course, who knows whether they would have won in 1984 if they had not boycotted in Los Angeles. So that is one of the most remarkable achievements by a men's team. The Soviet Union won one Olympic Games, two World Championships, and two World Cups. Five world tournaments in a row: 1977, 1978, 1980, 1981, 1982 is a pretty remarkable achievement. That team was again led by a pretty remarkable coach Viacheslav Platonov, one of the best coaches in the history of volleyball.

The U.S. started to get good about 1981 or 1982, which was about the time we had moved into a full-time training center. This young group of very talented Americans became available to us led by Karch Kiraly, Dusty Dvorak, Craig Buck, Pat Powers, and Steve Timmons, a legendary group. Slowly we crept up to the highest level of the world, and even though the USA finished thirteenth at the World Championships, they played the Soviet Union in our pool and played them as close a match as anybody did. We weren't quite ready to beat them, though. At that time Timmons and Powers were not yet playing for us, and Buck and Berzins were not full-time starters, so four players with world class skills were available in the Olympics and we still played them pretty well.

In 1983 we won the NORCECA Zone and in 1984 we took a tour of the Soviet Union, which was to be a pre-Olympic tour. We played the Soviet Union four or five matches and won them all. So we felt pretty good going into the Olympic Games. We had a streak of 28, 30, and then 32 straight wins heading into the Olympic Games in Los Angeles.

That 1984 team was also a model team in some respects. It was the first time that any team had received serve using only two of their players. We ran a very movement-oriented offense that a lot of people called the swing attack, where players went from one side of the court to the other based on some blocking match-ups. Some of our middle blockers wound up playing outside. We also did some match-up blocking. So, we did a lot of things that were used by other teams afterwards because of our success. (Editor's Note: Doug Beal was head men's National Coach during that period and designed those unique team strategies). That group basically won the 1983 Zones, the 1984 Olympic Games, the 1985 World Cup, the 1986 World Championships, and the 1988 Olympic Games. It kind of matched what the Russians did in terms of winning five consecutive world events. The U.S. team from 1983-1988 was voted at the Centennial mark of the sport as one of the top three teams of all time. The team that actually got voted "the best" was the Italian team, even though they never won an Olympic Games!

As we go through the history of the Olympics, the 1992 Barcelona Olympics was won by Brazil. It was the only Olympics that Brazil won until the new millenium. One of the unique things about Brazil is that they are the only men's team that has participated in every single Olympic tournament since 1964. The only one they won was the tournament in Barcelona in 1992. It was a very young team that peaked at just the right moment. Certainly being American and being biased, if the U.S. team had had Kiraly, I think we would have won our third

Olympics in a row, to be the only men's team that would have won three. We finished third, losing to Brazil in a pretty close match in the semi-finals 3-1. That team included Timmons, Partie, and Stork. Brazil was only on the top of the world for that very short period. They didn't win anything in 1991, they didn't win anything in 1993, and so it was a quick blip up and down.

Just after that 1992 Olympic Games, and actually even before 1992, starting in 1989, the Italians started to dominate the world. In 1989, Italy won the World Cup, beating Cuba in the finals. In 1990, Italy won the World Championships. So Italy was actually favored going into the Olympic Games. The U.S. beat Italy in our pool and Italy lost in the quarter-finals to a Dutch team that had their first string setter injured, so it was a big upset. The Dutch team beat the Russians and wound up playing in the finals against Brazil. Brazil beat them really badly. The U.S. then beat Cuba for third place. Italy lost that Olympic tournament in kind of an upset. Italy won the 1994 World Championships again in Greece. So, that was Italy's second World Championships in a row.

In 1996, Italy was favored again to win the Olympic Games in Atlanta and they lost a really close five-game match to Holland. So, this was Holland's little blip on the landscape. The only year that Holland was number one was 1996, because of the Olympic championship. Again this was a five-game match. 1998 was another World Championship for Italy, winning their third World Championships in a row, which I think is another "unprecedented achievement." In 1999 the World Cup was held and Russia won, but in a very close match. In 2000, Italy was favored to win the Olympic Games again and lost in the semi-finals to Yugoslavia, who goes on to win the Olympic Games. Again, while strong, Italy fell short of winning it all.

This Italian team, in terms of longevity, is felt by many to be the best team in the history of men's volleyball. The coach was Julio Velasco for most of that period. He had outstanding players which included a middle blocker, Andrea Gardini, an opposite who was also a super star named Andrea Zorzi, and Andrea Giani who played a lot of positions-middle, outside, and opposite. So they had some pretty remarkable players who played many years, but they never won an Olympic Games.

Meanwhile, Brazil began its domination of the new century, by winning most World Leagues and the Olympic title in 2004. Our USA men made the medal round in Athens, only to lose to both Brazil, the Gold medalists, and Russia the Bronze medal winners. Brazil's domination of the World League, winning most the titles in the last decade, has seen them also return to the Olympic Gold medal stand in 2004. They were dislodged at the 2008 Beijing Olympics by the core of the 2004 USA team, which, under the leadership of Hugh McCutcheon, won the Gold without losing a match. This was despite personal tragedy in the loss of his father-in-law and injuries to his mother-in-law. That meant Ron Larsen, the assistant, head coached the team for the first three matches. This was truly a feat of a strong team, along with a strong program, working together beyond reproach to win the Gold!

Professional Volleyball

On the men's side, professional and club volleyball is basically synonymous. In the rest of the world they call it club volleyball. The professional world is dominated by Europe. The number one country is clearly Italy. Their professional league has been growing and has been successful for over fifty years. Most of the top players in the world, regardless of what country they come from, have been through the Italian league at one point or another. The U.S. players started to go to Italy back in the '70's and one of the very first to go there was Kirk Kilgore. His team played in Rome and won Italian championships before Kilgore was injured in a training accident in late fall of 1975, which left him a quadriplegic. Kilgore was still in a Rome hospital when the U.S. team played in a tournament in Rome in January of 1976. A number of us who knew him and played with him went to visit him. He was in an iron lung and had not yet been diagnosed with the severity of a spinal cord injury and was about to be transferred to a rehab hospital in the United States. Kilgore was probably the first successful player that traveled to Europe to play professional volleyball. Then a number of U.S. national players started going later in the '70's and continuing through the '80's and to the current period.

The group of U.S. players that really opened the door for a whole lot of Americans to play professionally abroad, were the players on the '84 Olympic team who began going over with Dusty Dvorak who went in 1986. Along with Dvorak were Dave Saunders, Pat Powers, Craig Buck, Steve Timmons, Karch Kiraly, Doug Partie and Bob Ctvrlik—indeed almost all the top players from the 1984 and 1988 Olympic men's team wound up playing in Italy at one point or another. Some played for quite a while and almost all of them very successfully. They played many years, and even up to today, American players are very coveted by a lot of the Italian professional Volleyball clubs. The league in Italy is certainly the most commercially successful one in the world, as well as the oldest league.

Professional volleyball has made several efforts to get established in the United States. By far, the most successful effort was the IVA (International Volleyball Association), which ran from 1975-81. It was a regional league with teams mostly in the southwest, although they had franchises at one time or another in Denver, Salt Lake and Seattle, but principally southern California and Arizona. There was also a coed league with two women on the court at one time. Some of the franchises were quite successful and played in the summer.

People would rather not go indoors in the summer, although they tried to fit it in where it could be fit in. It had some pretty substantial backing at the time and some of the franchises did quite well. They wound up with quite a few foreign players from Brazil and Europe. A lot of U.S. players obviously played as well. League President, television producer, David Wolper became ill, and his doctor advised him to drop out of all of his business endeavors immediately. When that happened equally talented television people like Barry Diller and Berry Gordy elected to go on to other projects more directly in their field. But I thought the effort was quite creative and it had some high points, including one of the league's superstars, basketballer Wilt Chamberlin, who greatly enjoyed playing the sport of volleyball.

The other efforts that professional volleyball in the United States has had have been on the women's side. There have been at least two women's leagues, though neither in my view, have been nearly as successful as the IVA. There was a women's league called Major League Volleyball (MLV), which was in the Midwest mostly, although there was also a San Jose franchise and a New York franchise. It didn't draw spectators very well and lasted three or four years back in the mid '80's. There have been a couple of very small efforts at women's leagues.

However, around the world, professional volleyball is doing quite well. It is very strongly established in Brazil and is successful in Argentina, so it certainly has a foothold in South America—particularly Brazil. There is a strong league that has been operating for a number of years in Japan that is done very professionally and very well. Almost every country in Europe, western and eastern, has a professional league of some type with Italy being by far the most successful and the most enduring with the longest history and the greatest tradition. They experience lots of television coverage, very enthusiastic fan support, and great media coverage in the sporting papers. Other countries are pretty good as well. Greece has developed quite an excellent league. Spain, France, Germany, Holland, and a number of the Eastern European countries are improving quite a lot with Poland perhaps being the leader of that group.

The continued growth of professional volleyball has the challenge of a conflict in scheduling between the international events that are conducted by the international federations and the various professional leagues, which are each conducted by the specific country's federations or an organization that is solely responsible for the league itself. There is constantly this pull on the players to either play professionally or play in the league and the scheduling conflict that is presented to them makes it very difficult to do both. At some point in the near future we have to resolve that hurdle, if our sport is to continue its tremendous growth.

The women's game has seen remarkable growth, in part due to Title IX, with 400,000 high school girls playing in the USA currently, and some 180,000 Junior Olympians from ten-eighteen years old. With nearly 10,000 scholarships for females at the collegiate level, it has a strong success at the Olympic level as well, with Silver medals in 1984 and 2008, and a Bronze in 1992. NCAA Final Fours for women recently have had sell out crowds of over 15,000 fans, and every state in the union but one has high school varsity programs (compared to just twenty-two for the boys).

Hugh McCutcheon has been joined by none other than Karch Kiraly to see if they can take the Lang Ping led Silver medal women's team from 2008, to a first Gold medal in 2012. The years of leadership by the national team head coaches like Arie Selinger, Terry Liskevych, Mick Haley, Dr. Gary Sato, Toshi Yoshida and the amazing Chinese star player and coach Lang Ping, will give them a great foundation on which to stand to reach this new plateau.

CHAPTER 4

U.S. and International Beach Volleyball

by Sinjin Smith, President of the FIVB Beach Volleyball World Council

While Beach Volleyball was born in Honolulu, Hawaii in 1915, this unique sport started its first growth spurt in Southern California in the '30's and '40's. The next strong growth period was in the mid '50's to mid '60's, when two teams proved to be dominant in matches from Northern California down to Brazil. In the finals of most tournaments were defensive wonders Gene Selznick and Ron Lang pitied against the tall bombers, Mike O'Hara and Mike Bright. As with champions John McEnroe Vs. Bjorn Borg in tennis, four decades later, these hot and explosive matches created enthusiastic fans identifying with each team, and soon the Manhattan Beach Wimbledon World Championship of Beach Volleyball, drawing between 10,000 and 15,000 excited fans to each final day contest. While Selznick and Lang played over a longer period of time and won more total tournaments, O'Hara and Bright won the first five World Tournaments at Manhattan Beach, (a record that still stands today), with Selznick and Lang winning the sixth annual tournament in 1965.

By the late '70s, because of the crowds the sport was attracting, sponsors began to put up prizes and eventually even a bit of prize money. This eventually led to local television coverage so sponsors could secure more mileage ("eyeballs") and thereby leverage their investment. Then it was off to the races and a fight to own those professional events.

Promoters were successfully putting on events and making money and receiving too many benefits compared to the players.

37

Sinjin Smith

Players decided to follow the advice of a professional sports agent and allowed him to set up a player's organization that would eventually run the whole sport. This turned out to benefit the players in a big way as they were making decisions about their sport and really began to make substantial prize money. This did not mean that the players were treated like professionals, as many people thought of Beach Volleyball as a sport for beach bums and this was particularly true outside of California.

The mid '80s brought exposure of Beach Volleyball to the rest of the country with television coverage and also new volleyball tournaments in other parts of the country. There was not much knowledge of the sport outside of California. Now, though, with a professional organization and corporate sponsors coming to the game to attach their name to this lifestyle event, television became even more interested and began to televise the sport countrywide. This exposure helped the public realize that the athletes who played this game at the highest level were professionals and they were starting to receive the same kind of respect as athletes from the mainstream sports.

The whole country was now aware of the sport of volleyball and even the stars who played it. Because of this exposure you could watch a game in many parts of the country. They first started to play in Florida and then the east coast and along the Great Lakes and before we knew it, every state in the country was playing in the sand. It didn't matter that there wasn't a beach because they would haul in the sand and pretend they were in sunny California. For many that was the closest they would ever get to California but that was just fine. If these young players from outside of California wanted to try to break into the professional ranks then they would end up moving to the west coast to train against the best and test their skills. Universities such as UCLA, USC, and Stanford began to award scholarships, and the growth of volleyball continued.

Also by the mid '80s, the sport now had greater interest from other countries such as Brazil and Italy. They wanted to take advantage of the success that the USA was experiencing on the beach. Many countries outside of the USA already had great success with the indoor game of volleyball played with six on a side but a group of forward thinking promoters wanted to take advantage of the tremendous commercial possibilities and unique appeal of the beach game. These countries put on their own events and immediately achieved great success, with big crowds and television and sponsor support.

The international governing body of the sport of volleyball, FIVB, recognized the value of Beach Volleyball and took control of all international competitions. This was the beginning of the FIVB Beach Volleyball World Tour with events on every continent. Some of the countries with major international events were, of course, Brazil and Italy, but also Argentina, Japan, China, South Africa, Russia, France, Germany, Spain, Korea, Switzerland, Belgium, Puerto Rico, Mexico, Canada, Australia, Norway, and USA. By allowing two men or women volleyballers to travel and rent a hotel room for four days, all at their own expense, in order to compete for prize money of varying amounts—usually totalling $150,000 per tournament gave each hosting city a superb, highly televised event to show off their city. By the early '90s, the USA had a multi-million dollar tour with network television coverage and if you really searched, you could also find national tours in several other countries offering some prize money. The FIVB had also successfully accomplished developing a successful world tour and realized that this sport was a perfect Olympic Sport because almost any country could afford to develop a two men or two women team. It would take much more than that, though, to become an Olympic Sport.

USA Women take top three spots in World Tour. Photo courtesy of FIVB

Immediately following the highly successful 1984 Los Angeles Olympic Games Mike O'Hara, who had served as the Organizing Committee's Executive Director of Sports, traveled to the annual meeting of the FIVB, international body for World Volleyball, representing the United States Volleyball Association. While the initial response to his recommendation that beach players be invited into the FIVB included the term "beach bums," he was able to motivate their dynamic leader, FIVB President Rubin Acosta, to accompany him to Rio de Janeiro, Brazil, to witness first hand this unique, exciting new sport. His reaction was immediate, and totally positive. Months later Acosta replied affirmatively to O'Hara's request that O'Hara represent the FIVB in talking to his International Olympic Committee President Juan

Antonio Samaranch and his "brothers" in his home city of Barcelona, Spain, about making Beach Volleyball a part of the Olympic Games. That concept was accepted initially as a "demonstration sport" at the next Olympics in Barcelona in 1992. Since President Samaranch was a native of Barcelona, home of fabulous beaches, O'Hara received his enthusiastic support! The Barcelona Organizing Committee settled for holding the beach competition in another beach city, two weeks after the formal close of the Games, and the crucial initial entry permission as a demonstration sport was obtained.

As the result of that initial exposure, the IOC and the Atlanta Organizing Committee for the 1996 Olympic Games were convinced by the President of the FIVB that Beach Volleyball would be a great success for them. This would have been almost an impossible feat but with the power of the FIVB President, Ruben Acosta, anything was possible.

Beach Volleyball would make its full fledged debut in 1996 in Atlanta and enjoy enormous success. It was one of the first sports to have all its event tickets sell out to the public which surprised everyone but the people who were close to this dynamite sport. A crowd of 10,000 spectators showed up for each of the two event sessions per day, for ten days, to watch the best teams from around the world fight for the Gold medal. The American men's team and the Brazilian women won the Gold medals on the beach. This didn't surprise many in the volleyball world, but the changes were coming fast as the sport continued to develop internationally. It would take another four years and another great success at the 2000 Olympics in Sydney before the IOC would decide to make Beach Volleyball a permanent addition to the Olympic program. This time it would be the Australian women and a new ninth-ranked American men's team winning the Gold medals and previously neither of those specific sport teams had won an international event! The sport had truly come of age and was open to the world. Since then Misty May and Kerri Walsh have won back to back Gold medals in the 2004 and 2008 Olympics, and

Phil Dalhauser joined partner Todd Rogers on the Gold medal platform in Beijing for the USA men.

Phil Dalhauser and Todd Rogers, 2008 Olympic and 2008 Olympic Gold medalists. Photo courtesy of FIVB

Misty May and Kerri Walsh, 2004 Gold medalists and World Champions Photo courtesy of FIVB

Due to the tremendous popularity of the women's indoor sport, most people in the USA before the '70s thought of volleyball as a women's sport. This was because of all of the existing women's programs in all level schools and the lack of those programs for the men. Things have changed considerably since that time. When Beach Volleyball became professional, sponsors were willing to pay more for the men than the women and you would see more men's events and more prize money offered to the men. This was true not only in the USA but also in international beach tournaments world wide. Today you see a different story starting at the top. The Olympics has an equal number of men's and women's teams competing. The world tour now has the same number of men's events as women's events and they have equal prize money as well. The USA has moved in the same direction with its national tour that has men's and women's events offering the same number of events and the same prize money. We have seen other countries following this example and moving in the same direction.

Because of this boom in the sport there is now a tremendous number of places to play sand volleyball all over our country and throughout the world. Not only does just about every public beach in California have courts available, but the same holds true for most of the country. You will find courts all over the east coast and on the Great Lakes open for public play and now in many parks around the country you can find areas dedicated to sand volleyball. Many parts of the country where bowling and softball were the after work activities connected to local bars, there has been a transition to sand volleyball. They are able to play men's or women's or mixed volleyball games at all different skill levels in a relatively small area. Many of the colleges and universities are also putting up sand volleyball courts on their campuses.

You may wonder what many of these hard core players do during the winter in cold weather areas. They found a solution so that they can play all the year around, even if it is snowing. There are many indoor sand facilities that can hold several courts. These are very popular for playing at night as well. So now if you want to play Beach Volleyball anywhere in the country during anytime of the year, you can usually find a venue with all these places to play across the country. You can also find many people willing to teach players to play, from kids to grownups, and at all levels of play. It is common to see the professional volleyballers' names attached to clinics across the country, not only for those wanting to learn the game but also those wanting to get up close and personal with the male and/or female athletes.

If you had told me twenty-four years ago when I started playing on the beach in Southern California that Beach Volleyball would be an Olympic sport and professional not only in the USA but in many other countries as well, with a strong professional World Tour with top teams from every continent, I would have said you were crazy! I know differently today and believe that anything is possible for this attractive sport in the future.

CHAPTER 5

The Magic of Four Woman Volleyball

By Gabrielle Reece

Lucky for me I moved from the Caribbean to Florida my Junior year of high school. I dabbled in volleyball while growing up in the Islands, but did not get serious until I moved to St. Petersburg at the age of fifteen. When you are 6'3" at that age it is just expected you know how to play volleyball and basketball. Believe me I didn't.

Fast forward to me signing my letter of intent to play for Florida State University at the last moment possible (I believe in the month of May or June). Coach Randy Dagostino taught me middle blocking steps eight weeks before I headed off to attend FSU and play for Cecile Reynaud. That's how green I really was.

I always admit to the fact of learning how to play certain parts of the game while in college. Oftentimes I felt like I was fudging it. The good news was I am coachable and big. I did well at FSU, but not without a lot of humbling lessons (both on the court and in life). Cecile was a brilliant mentor to me, and stressed personal responsibility.

When I left FSU I had fallen in love with the game and everything around it. Practice, my teammates, discipline, working hard, and feeling like you had to earn it, and not that things would be handed to you. Remember, simultaneously to playing in college I started a modeling career out of New York that was a completely contrary universe to sports.

I moved to Miami after college and started playing two on two in the sand. I was a true middle so passing and setting skills were a whole new world to me. There were thirty-five year old, 5 foot 8 inches women running me all over the place kicking my butt. What kind of volleyball was this? Long story short, an encouraging and wonderful woman named Barbara Beirman told me I should move to California to attempt to play professionally. She and I had gone to Puerto Rico and gotten killed in a WPVA event where our first match was against Brazilian superstar Jackie Silva. I'm not sure she even broke a sweat.

At the age of twenty-two I packed up my stuff and headed out west. I had become close to an AVP athlete by the name of Dan Vrebolovich who helped me get settled once I arrived.

Holly McPeak invited me to practice where I was able to be a practice dummy for her and whichever partner she was playing with at the time. An athlete is fortunate when they get to practice every day with players more experienced than themselves. Holly is tough, hard working, and I knew I should just try and soak up as much of it as I could.

I competed in a few WPVA events, and then got word that they were creating a four on four beach tour and would I be open to being drafted? I was the first pick in the draft by Team Paul Mitchell in this new Bud Light tour run by Craig Elledge. The tour was sprinkled with USA players, and All Americans.

For a new beach player, but experienced indoor player, this game was heaven. The number of adjustments you had to make were minimal (good side, bad side, the wind etc). Not to mention I enjoyed the combination of being on the beach, with the quick play, and team-like atmosphere. The four on four men's and women's game survived for many years and did really well for its television partner ESPN. The fact that Anheiser Busch was our headlining sponsor didn't hurt (they at the time spent a lot of money on it).

At the end of the day no matter how much I love the game of volleyball it still needs to work as a business. In the late 1980's and early '90's when the sport was growing led by Sinjin, Randy Stoklos, and Karch the mistake was we were not consolidated playing together. The women's doubles was on the WPVA, the men were on the AVP, and then there were those of us on the fours. It's almost as if all of our efforts to grow the sport were so fractionalized we couldn't get the maximum benefit.

Once all of the male and female doubles athletes were playing for the AVP we tried twice to bring back the four on four game with them to no avail. Initially this could only be done by doing exhibitions with the hope of rolling out a complete summer schedule if things worked. Needless to say we have tried three times and now the sport is just struggling to survive. My feeling is that Beach Volleyball is a niche sport that has to compete with the traditional ball and stick sports. With a tough economy and a floundering platform it's challenging. I often wonder, but why is it always one of the most popular sports at the Olympics? That seems to be the one time people get a real feel for the magic of the beach game. The amazing athletes, the sun, the beach, and if you are lucky, the water. There is nothing like it. The dominance of Misty May and Kerri Walsh also contributed hugely to the popularity of the sport via the Olympic Games.

Most beach players play the traditional six on six indoor game that then lead them to the beach. My hopes were that four on four could be a part of the original two on two beach tour. Fours could then become a great introduction for so many talented indoor players. Tennis has doubles and singles, and I never understood why we didn't have both doubles and fours together. Athletes could then choose to continue to play fours, or like so many successful fours players (Elaine Youngs, Jenny Jordan, and Annette Davis, to name a few) go on to doubles. There are talented indoor players that really don't have an opportunity to enter the beach game easily. If you think the game of two on two is easy to play just because you know how to play six on six it's an entirely different beast. It is one that oftentimes intimidates or scares off potentially great players who lack experience.

I myself don't believe I could have been an authentic ambassador for the game of volleyball if I did not have the opportunity to play four on four. This discipline was well suited for my style of play. Not to mention the fact that the first time I picked up a beach ball was at the age of twenty- two. I wasn't from California, growing up on the beaches playing. I wouldn't have been able to afford the number of years it would have taken me to get really good at doubles. I would have had to find another occupation.

I hope I get to see the day when the efforts of the sport of volleyball are united, and there is a tour where young, talented athletes can make a healthy living.

I always say that the game saved me—first with the chance to go to college on a scholarship, and then with the valuable lessons I learned throughout my career. The places I have traveled, the coaches I have learned from, the players I have been fortunate to play with and against, and the life I built from the foundation of sport has been fabulous.

Gabby Reece

Michael O'Hara's comments about Gabrielle Reece: *Back in the '90's, I was fascinated by the way a gorgeous 6'3" beautifully coordinated and proportioned athlete nicknamed Gabby, from Florida, was constantly being photographed, either on the volleyball court, or modeling, or hanging out with the beautiful people. When she fell in love with the beach game, and found that she could match up with the four women game, it began to achieve better viewership numbers, and sponsorship followed.*

Her move to the west coast afforded her access to many micro-phones and typewriters, and she became an even more effective advocate for the four woman game. Fans in the television crowd began to see that the defense put up a more equal two or three woman block, and the backcourt diggers became more effective, yielding the important LONGER RALLIES. It also gave women viewers a chance to see beautiful women in athletic costume, and afforded the males the opportunity to see twice as many attractive women flying around the court with reckless abandon.

About that time, Mike Miazga, at that time Editor in Chief of *Volleyball Magazine* in 2006, conducted their thirty year celebration poll, asking members of the sports community who they felt were the most recognizable athletes in the game. "Gabby" Reece, after superstar Gold medal winning Olympians Karch Kiraly, Misty May-Treanor and Kerri Walsh finished, first second and third respectively and Gabby was sixth!

Gabby continues to motivate anyone that will listen, concerning the terrific asset value and attractiveness of her favorite sport, and it would not surprise me at all if she were to unveil an international version of her four woman sport sometime soon.

Gabby Reece

Gabby Reece

CHAPTER 6

Rules For Indoor and Beach Volleyball

by Dr. James Coleman

On July 7, 1896, ten men demonstrated the game called "Mintonette" at the Springfield YMCA School. John Lynch, the Holyoke Fire Chief and J. Curren, the Holyoke Mayor, were team captains for the match. These two men along with Morgan and physician Frank Wood helped to formulate the rules and develop the game of Mintonette. Professor Alfred T. Halstead, an observer of this first demonstration game and a faculty member of the School for Christian Workers, remarked that it appeared that the men were "volleying the ball back and forth over the net." Morgan adopted Halstead's suggestion that the game be called "volley ball." The only change today is that the name is now one word, "volleyball." The original court was fifty feet by twenty-five divided into two equal halves of twenty-five x twenty-five by a net which was six feet six inches high. The court size was adaptable depending on the space available. The ball was a rubber basketball bladder and not too different in size and weight from today's volleyball.

The server stood with one foot on the back line and batted the ball over the net with one hand. A player on the server's team could "help" the ball across the net on service. A server continued to serve until being "put out" because the server's team did not win the rally. If the server's team won the rally, the team won a point. The game was divided into innings, similar to baseball. Three servers being "put out" ended an "inning" and entitled the opponent to serve. Touching the net or catching the ball was illegal. A ball could rebound off the ceiling or walls and remain in play. Dribbling the ball (consecutive hits by the same

51

player), was allowed. There have been four principal eras of rules development in the United States. The approximate dates of these eras are:
- The initial rules: 1896-1912. These rules were modified in many cities and regions around the country. The modifications caused the game to become quite diverse.
- The Harry Schmidtt combined rules: 1912-1928. Schmidtt, a student at George Williams College, attempted to standardize the rules around the United States.
- The United States Volleyball Association Rules: 1928-1964.
- The International Rules: 1964-present.

The USVBA gave organizational structure to the study and legislation of the rules. There is not as much study of the rules today as in former years, but there is a very strong attempt to use the same rules as the rest of the world. The rules today are dynamic and are being changed to make volleyball a more exciting and marketable game. The International Rules Era led to five major changes that improved the game:

1. Beginning in 1965, the blockers were allowed to reach over the net to block the ball.
2. Starting in 1977, the touch on the block did not count as the first of the three ball contacts by a team converting defensive play into an offensive play.
3. Beginning in 1989 the deciding game of a match was played to 15 points using the rally scoring system, conceived and proposed to the FIVB Rules Committee by Michael O'Hara. In the rally scoring system, a point is scored on each rally. After the Gold medal men's indoor volleyball finals at the 1996 Atlanta Olympics, both coaches wrote to the FIVB Rules Committee requesting all future competition games to include the Rally Scoring System. Their match had lasted over three hours, and before the match was finished many spectators left the stadium.
4. Beginning in 1998, all games were played by the use of rally scoring, with Beach Volleyball being the last to adopt the system. Normally games are played to twenty-five

points except in the deciding game, which is still to 15 points. All games must be won by a minimum of two points.

5. A Libero player is allowed to be used. The word Libero is Italian for "free" which indicates somewhat the nature of the position. The Libero player has some very complex rules, but simply is allowed to enter the game only as a back row player. The Libero cannot serve, block, or attack. The Libero cannot overhand set the ball from in front of the three meter line. Libero is only a serve receiver and defensive player. The Libero may enter the game an unlimited number of times for any back row player, but must sit out one rally between exiting and re-entering the game.

A Libero is designated by wearing a different color jersey than the rest of the team. This difference in color of jersey is used for score keeping purposes and allows the Libero to run on and off the court, in front of the end line but behind the three meter line, without having to go through traditional substitution procedure. Even though today's volleyball is as versatile regarding playing conditions as the original game of volleyball, there are only two major types of volleyball played in international competition and in the Olympic Games. These are six player "volleyball" and two player "Beach Volleyball" "Volleyball." is normally played indoors on a hard surface and "Beach Volleyball" is normally played outdoors on sand.

2009 World Men's Beach Volleyball Championships, Norway. Photo courtesy of FIVB

Generally the six person game requires the players to occupy specific positions on the court at the time of the service, requires them to rotate to all six court positions and allows for substitutions. The beach game allows non-rotation and no substitutions. In the six person game there are restrictions placed on the "back row players," whereas the doubles game does not discriminate between the players. The precise rules for these games are published by the United States Volleyball Association. Although the original game of volleyball was created for men, women began to show interest in volleyball as early as 1914. Almost immediately a separate set of rules began to develop among the women playing the game.

By 1916 the net was lowered to 7'6" where it remained until 1961 as the US began to move toward international rules and the current net height. In 1926 a Committee on Volleyball for Girls and Women was formed. Among the rules:

- Eight players on a team.
- Two trials for a service if the first were a "net" service.
- Any number of hits on one side of the net.
- No playing the ball twice in succession.
- Game of thirty minutes split by a five minute half.
- Net height of 7'6" (228.6cm).
- Net height for elementary girls of 6'6" (198 cm). Today, the rules for both men and women are the same. The only difference is the height of the net. The men's net is 2.43 meters (7'11 5/8") and the women's net is 2.23 meters (7'4 1/8"). The court is nine meters by eighteen meters (29'6" x 58').

The Rules Commission for Beach Volleyball experimented with a smaller court of eight meters by sixteen meters (26' 3" x 52' 6") for beach doubles, and made the change for the 2004 Olympics, international and national competition. The indoor court has a line parallel to the net and 3 meters (9' 10") from the centerline. Back row players must take off from behind this line in order to attack the ball. Back row players are not allowed to block. Serving may occur from any place behind the playing court in either indoor or beach volleyball. Today's most powerful serves travel at a velocity over 100 kilometers per hour. The perpetual conflict in the volleyball rules over the years has been

the interpretation of ball handling. In principle, the rules have prohibited "catching and throwing the ball." In fact, the legality of ball handling in both basketball and volleyball has been defined by "common practice."

As stated by both Lu and Flanagan, ball handling is an interpretation defined in practice by the referees. The fine line between a thrown ball and a legal contact cannot be defined on paper such that it can be interpreted precisely in practice by the

USA Women Triple Block 2009 World Grand Prix. Photo courtesy of FIVB

referees. This interpretation is in constant change. It will remain so for perpetuity. The great game of volleyball will continue to appeal to sportsmen of all ages because of its variety of forms. There will be the speed and power of the sensational athletes and the safety for the less skilled athletes. There will be the complexity of the offenses and defenses of the great teams and the simplicity of the game at the family picnics. Volleyball is truly a "miracle game."

CHAPTER 7

Youth and High School Volleyball

by John Kessel, USAV Director of Membership Development & Disabled Programs

Volleyball is a lifetime sport, but like any sport, the younger you can start to learn and experience it, the better you will be at it. As it is a non-contact sport, it is safe for kids to compete with and against adults. As it is a rebound game, but not using any sporting equipment to rebound with, it can be very challenging for a novice, of any age. There are Nationals for twelve and under kids, all the way up to seventy-five and over age groups. Perhaps most important is that the game, practices and matches, are great FUN!. This all takes place in a true team sport where no star can dominate without the supportive contacts of fellow players—developing cooperation all the time.

Everyone has played volleyball; from the beaches of southern California to the backyard picnic at Uncle Fred's, the ball has taken its fair share of spikes as well as slam dunks. The sport, when played under the international rules set by the FIVB, rules that essentially all good youth and high school aged players use, bears little resemblance to the battle by the barbecue. Volleyball and those who seek to excel within the sport truly fit the word amateur, which comes from French and Latin words for lover, for they do it because they love the sport.

Exposure to the game as played at the top levels nationally and internationally is a must for all, players and coaches alike, who wish to be a success in what some call "power volleyball." Every chance a player gets, he or she should watch the volleyball on television, or at levels well above his or her abilities. A great amount of learning takes place by watching and imitating. In any case, to play under the rules means one must know the FIVB rules and interpretations, which is a book in and unto itself. Adaptations of these governing rules by national bodies such as the National High School Federation, or even on a smaller scale, the local park and recreation departments, require further study by those teams who play under such adaptations. The rules themselves, therefore, are found in your league's governing rulebook. With the yearly evolution that occurs therein, all players and coaches must keep abreast of the latest rule developments in order to keep training proper skills and competing at the highest level possible.

The following fundamental and unique concepts should be understood by all participants as they grapple with playing volleyball "by the rules." As skills improve, the following concepts never change; factors that make the sport so dang hard to learn . . . INDOOR VOLLEYBALL.

Rebounding—All other key American sports allow you to pause or hold onto the ball. Since each team has three touches, they attempt, with each "pass" to position the ball where one of the three spikers will have an ideal opportunity to smash the ball to the opponent's floor! All other key American sports allow the player to pause or hold onto the ball, but volleyball does not.

Range of Play—From "a pancake," a finger height off the floor, to sky ball serves.

Ceiling Influence—Lights and beams may vary greatly.

Playing Area—Once the ball is served, the world is your court. You can pursue it anywhere, while making sure you don't get injured.

Court Surface—Sand, concrete, wood, grass, synthetic.

Congestion—On eighty-one square meters, six players must get along.

Body—Your whole body is your "racquet," while opponent contact is minimal.

Separation—Despite the congestion, actual physical contact is rare.

Varied Pace—The ball moves at continually varying and disparate speeds.

High Speed—Volleyballs, baseballs and hockey pucks go over 150 KPH.

Reaction Time—The defenders have the least amount of reaction time.

Transitions—There is no time to change squads from offense to defense.

Minimal Equipment—There really are no implements or pads required.

Unique Skills—Six pretty different additional skills, like well-trained and coordinated forearms.

Technique Rules—Every contact is judged and legal contact is up to each referee's interpretation.

Player Dominated—Americans are used to the coaching dominated styles seen on TV

High Skill Standards—We expect skill success percentages of 90-100%, not .300 or 50%.

Limited Coaching—Coaches are limited to two time outs and a limited number of substitutions.

Three Contacts—There can be a maximum of three contacts before your attack is completed.

Intermediate Contacts—Most sports have a final contact, like spiking the ball, that gets the glory.

Team Volleying—Played the way it is supposed to be, the sport is supposed to have rallies.

Rotation—After each change to a new server, one or more of the team rotates.

Unity—The team cannot depend on one player alone, winning teams don't gripe, they "batter the ball," since each team is allowed three contacts.

Defense/Offense Reversal—Defense scores the points, the offense stops them.

100% in the Air—The ball can touch the ground in almost any other sport, even tennis, but not ours.

Win by two, not one—25-24 or 15-14 wins most other

games, but not volleyball. You must win by two points. **You only get one chance to serve**—Other sports give you five trials or a second ball if you err.

Player Air Time—More time is spent in the air than any other sport. Jump serves, jump sets, 1-3 blockers, real and faking attackers all jump high as they can on every third contact and serve.

Let's take a look at the other ways kids can play the game—

Backyard Volleyball

The first place to play the game is in your own backyard or park. This is where kids can learn from adults, playing together. Attaching to a tree, house side wall or jungle gym, then anchoring at some distance to a pole is one way. While a net is preferred, just stringing up and playing over a rope is great fun. There is a tensioning knot, called a truckers knot by some, that uses a doubled back rope from the anchoring point through a loop tied into the rope itself, which allows for a pulley-like tightness. Court lines can be bought, but simply using corner markers of some sort such as socks or sandals also work fine.

Photo by John Kessel

There are great outdoor net systems available commercially, such as Park & Sun. These systems come complete with pre-marked court lines, three part poles, guy lines, stakes and even sand discs, and fit into a compact and durable duffle type bag. You can usually find these at the larger sporting goods stores, or online from any of the volleyball store web sites.

Backyard or not, the best way to learn the game is by actually touching the ball, rather than standing around watching others touch the ball. So at all levels, playing doubles, triples or a four person per side game, will result in faster learning and better range and movement by developing players. The game need not even be equal, such that two players (better skilled or not) can challenge themselves by playing three or four opponents on the other side.

The game as originated by William G. Morgan in 1895, was intended to be played one vs. one, two vs. two or three vs. three and more. Over one-hundred years later, this same small team size is still the best way for young kids to play the game. There are many options in smaller sided games, with smaller courts and lower net heights also allowed. Make variations that are fun, and let them spike early, from well off the net, and often. Lighter balls, bigger balls and other modified balls are used to keep the sting and weight of a normal adult ball during contact. Beach balls, balloons, and many other options are fun and fine. A racquetball court with a Wallyball net installed is another excellent court option, as the balls do not have to be chased as far when an error is made.

One vs. One—Played over a net or rope, the idea here is to learn not to rebound the ball back to the person who hits it at you, as if this skill were well learned you would be putting the ball back to the opponent (i.e., the person who hit it to you). Instead, you want to pass, and set to yourself, then hit the ball over the net, away from your opponent. It is better to learn first to keep the ball on your side of the net, rather than immediately directing the ball back to your opponent. This develops from the start with the three hits per side attitude that good teams use.

Players should work on not hitting the way they are facing, and also practice using their non-dominant hand. One handed ball control contact can also be developed. Court size can be three-four meters per sideline and endline.

Two vs. Two—This is the team size of the Olympic sport of Beach Volleyball. Playing doubles means once one player touches the first ball; the other player has a 100% chance of being the teammate who is to contact the second ball. If a player is a weak passer, the opponents serve that player, and he gets a lot of game like training on his weakness. If a player is the weaker attacker, that player will get most the serves so she has to spike the third ball, giving lots of practice to that weakness. And if a player is the weaker setter, opponents will serve her partner, so she gets lots of training on her setting weakness. Learning to cover the whole court with just one partner is a great experience in reading, anticipation and judgment. Court size ranges from four-six meters per side up to the Olympic standard of eight meters per sideline and endline. Grass courts are great options.

Kids' Beach and Grass Doubles. Photos by John Kessel

Three vs Three/Four vs. Four.—These games with smaller numbers of players on the court keep the play going by having more diggers/passers for the first contact, while still allowing each team player a higher chance of contacting the ball rather than watching. It is also fine to play unequal team sizes on a side, with three vs. four or two vs. three being fair and fine for learning. Court size is generally six meters to nine meters per sideline. The three person game can also be played on a three by nine meter court per side, playing full width of the net, with the endline being the normal court's three meter line. Setting up a rope court to go down the middle of a court is shown on the next page.

For more information, click on the "Grassroots" button on the USA Volleyball main web page. There, best practices, coaching information, parent and player information, posters, history of the game, sports quotes, and hundreds of articles are free of charge.

Photos by John Kessel

The best way to develop ball control is to cooperatively score. Traditional competitive scoring means the intent is to simply put the ball away against the opponent, either through your success, or their error. In cooperative scoring, the ball becomes the opponent, as both sides work together on ball control to see how many times they can contact it three times on a side, then volley the ball over—with each net crossing counting as a point.

U.S. Youth Volleyball League

The United States Youth Volleyball League has site locations which have expanded from California across the country. Their mission is to provide every child from age eight to fourteen a chance to learn and play volleyball in a fun, safe, supervised environment. One of the main tenets of the program is to encourage children to do their best with their abilities. With an emphasis on positive reinforcement, the program seeks to build confidence and self-esteem in each child. The program utilizes site directors, clinicians, and coaches who provide, through a structured curriculum, instruction and play. The USYVL is a family-oriented program where parents, siblings, grandparents, and friends are strongly encouraged to become involved. Parents and other volunteers assist with coaching, registration, check-in and equipment set-up.

For more information contact the USYVL:
12501 S. Isis Avenue Hawthorne, CA 90250
Phone: (310) 643-8398 Fax: (310) 643-8396
Toll-free Phone: 888.98.USYVL
E-mail: USYVL@aol.com

Volleyball Camps

No matter what an interested player's age, volleyball camps are excellent, intense, different and fun ways to gain new ideas and skills. Some camps are local, day only, and others are overnights, often held at colleges and universities, primarily in the summer. Either way, much like choosing a good club program, the best camps have good coaching, a ratio of one coach for every nine-twelve players maximum, and each group has their own full court. Some camps are just for teams, and others are "specialist" camps—focusing on the skills of hitting or setting for example, while still others will take any individual and teach them all the basic skills and team systems. USA Volleyball has a very extensive summer camp listing on its web site annually updated, while your local regional office and high school head coach will know of the best ones found closer to home. Additionally, your children's coaches would benefit greatly from attendance at a USAV Coaching Accreditation Program course, IMPACT or Level I, II, or III, so they learn the latest and best ways to teach athletes.

Junior Olympic Volleyball

Junior Olympic Volleyball age group programs have existed for over twenty-five years, for both boys and girls. They begin in many areas of the country at the ten and under age group, and have single age divisions all the way up to eighteen and under. Nearly 200,000 girls and boys compete annually for the chance to qualify their team into either the Club or Open divisions of the U.S. Junior Olympic Volleyball Championships, an event totaling over 1,000 teams, held annually in various parts of the nation. When you add in the National Qualifiers, which are spread throughout the nation geographically, a junior player gets to see the country from coast to coast. Thousands of local and regional events, generally November to June, help kids learn from under the guidance of great club programs and coaches. There are also season and national championships for U.S. Junior Olympic Beach Volleyball, the two vs. two game on sand, which is qualified for in some areas first on grass courts. See www.usavolleyball.org for information regarding the program nearest you.

Scholastic Volleyball

The first high school state championships? Many would guess it would be California back in the 1950s, but in fact they took place in 1932 in the state of Pennsylvania. During the past thirty years, volleyball has risen to become the second largest team sport for girls, after basketball. Over 400,000 girls play the game at the varsity level in nearly every high school in the nation. The opportunities at the junior high level, either inter-scholastically, on a more friendly level, or tournament-only basis, are equally large. This popularity for girls' volleyball repeats at the collegiate level, where the sport of volleyball offers the second largest scholarship opportunity of all sports.

In all but a handful of states, high school volleyball takes place in the fall, in various divisions based on school enrollment size. Even the smallest of schools will field a team, with prac-tices starting in August and ending in mid fall with regionals fol-lowed by the State Championships. It also is a great lead in sport to basketball, with all the jumping and defensive skills play-ers perform. Given the uniqueness of the sport, those girls get-ting the early start of junior high and/or Junior. Olympic program play, have a much stronger chance of making their high school team.

While world-wide the game showcases more males than females playing the game, in the USA this is not the case. Due to the popularity of the major American pro sports for men, starting with football, volleyball for boys is only found in less than half the states, and even at the Junior Olympic Volleyball level, is played by roughly one tenth the number of boys than girls. USA Volleyball has a grant program to help grow boys, teams and leagues, contact info@usav.org.

Coed Options

One of the more special aspects of the sport is that it is also played coeducationally, including a national championship level. This includes normal coed (three males, three females on a men's height net), as well as reverse coed (playing women only in the front row and men passing/digging and attacking from behind the three meter line on a women's height net). There is a USA National Coed Championships for various skill levels as the culminating finals for teams, and it is a very popu-lar option in most city parks and recreation programs. Since the game is non-contact, skilled young females have no problem playing with males. Similarly, skilled kids can easily play with adults, and the faster nature of the game with older players helps speed up the skill level and development of kids.

Practice and Compete on Different Surfaces.

One of the great things about the game is that it can be played on any surface. Grass, wood, sand, asphalt, court tiles, and concrete are all possible. The game is played outside in the snow at ski areas, with the kids wearing snow or ski boots, while another fun kid friendly version is to play in the pool, stringing the net/rope across the water to volley over. In Alaska and other well forested areas, volleyball enthusiasts play on wood chips. The Olympic discipline of Beach Volleyball is the most prominent example of this form of cross training.

CHAPTER 8

Training Methods and Strategy Differences Between Indoor and Beach Volleyball

by Gary Sato, D.C., Assistant USA Men's
National Team Coach

In all sports there is a rule of "specificity in training." This requires one to create or recreate an environment as similar to the real thing as possible. For Beach Volleyball, train two vs. two on the SAND with the wind, sun and other elements such as the correct ball, net height, antennaes, court dimensions, scoring system and rules. Also do the majority of your running and jump training on the SAND to most quickly attain your "SAND LEGS."

While Indoor Volleyball is played on the hardwood floor or Sport court with six vs. six and OUTDOOR with two vs. two, the basic tenet of PASS-SET-HIT and error free plays are consistent to both. Since preparation is the key to success, skills and drills performed with lots of repetitions of P-S-H is a great place to start. Then move on to defensive skills such as blocking/digging and coordinating the two as well as the all important TRANSITION from offense to defense and defense to offense. Transition demands lots of communication especially with six players on the court with everyone doing their part and lots of points can be scored by teams that transition well.

Beach Volleyball players require good all around skills but specialization does occur with each player usually favoring the left side or right side of the court. On defense specialization occurs where one player may do a majority of the blocking and the other will defend the parts of the court, as they see what their blocking player leaves open for the rest of the players to cover.

The INDOOR game has evolved to a game of complex specialization. Most teams employ an offense called a 5-1 where there are five hitter/blocker types and one setter. A few of the hitter/blockers are also required to be skillful at passing and some teams will utilize a new player position called a LIBERO which is a backcourt specialist limited to passing and back court defense and may substitute only in the back row, but for any player. In addition the Libero may not attack above the net or hand set from in front of the three meter line.

USAV clinic session.

The basic strategies are the same taking all variables into account such as your strengths/weaknesses, the other teams strengths/weaknesses, habitual tendencies and how you may "match-up" against them. For example if you have information that a certain player is not good at serve reception you may have your players serve that person as often as possible to gain an advantage by outright error or causing the pass and set to be "off the net" which limits their attacking options. Another example would be if a team has a favorite player that gets a high percentage of kills and attacks it a certain way you can line up your best blockers in front of them and dig around the block hoping to stop or slow down this tendency. If playing on the beach one must be aware of the WIND direction at all times using it help you and not hurt you as you make your ball placement and contact decisions.

It has also been said that "an ounce of prevention is worth a pound of cure" and a well-conditioned volleyball player can decrease his chances for injury and increase their chances for success by performing a pre-season overall training program. Such a program would prepare the athlete for the extreme physical demands of the sport with an emphasis on the legs and shoulders (especially the spiking arm). Adequate core strengthening, stretching program and shoulder gym exercises should be done everyday to help balance the wear and tear of a long season. Proper nutrition and rest are also important factors as well as a great attitude. Be sure to get any injuries checked out by the appropriate people immediately to prevent them from getting worse. Do all of these things and you can be at your very best when the whistle blows. Good luck!

Men's Recreational play. Photo by John Kessel

CHAPTER 9

Volleyball Clothing and Equipment

by Michael O'Hara

Clothing for volleyball comes in two separate categories: one for indoor and grass play and one for beach and pool play. The common ingredient for both categories is comfort. While each team needs to wear the same uniform, with different numbers, during competition, even those motives point toward comfort and appearance.

For all casual play or scrimmage on the beach, trunks or shorts and a tee shirt carry the day. The type of style statement made is as personal and customized as the length of the trunks, shirt color, etc. The addition of a golf shirt might even score major points.

Indoor practice apparel requires the same type of decision making process. However, the crucial additional element for grass, asphalt, and indoor wood surfaces concerns the footwear utilized. While most of the major shoe companies produce an excellent line of footwear designed especially for volleyball, some stress sturdy, foot protecting features, while others, including some of the finest Japanese manufacturers, put forth a lighter, higher jumping product. In addition to this basic decision, the style features of the different shoe lines tend to be the other major decision making factor.

The main accessories for volleyball players on all surfaces involve the knees and ankles. Since volleyball is such a vertical sport, with lots more jumping than running, many players find that the knee joints are tested the most, with the ankles a close second. All kinds of supportive wraps and bracing products are available, when and if needed.

USA Men's Team in World League Action. Photo courtesy of FIVB

On hard surfaces, a padded knee wrap also becomes a handy buffer, should the athlete decide to dive for the ball. Since the hard surface volleyball player spends a lot of time jumping and landing, thick, sweat absorbing socks are an essential. A comfortable sweat suit is important for the proper initial warming of body muscles, as well as the crucial cooling down after a workout or match. Of equal import is proper stretching both before and after each competition.

In America, the equipment needed to enjoy the sport of volleyball is minimal. The availability of poles, nets and balls in parks, beaches and schools, usually available to the public on given hours, and days and nights, make the pursuit of this type of healthy fun very accessible. Where it is necessary to bring your own equipment, the poles holding up the volleyball net must be round and smooth and be inserted securely into the ground. The wires or rope below head height should not be used to secure the posts. The posts should be put up between 0.5 meter and 1 meter from the court.

The ball is round, with a circumference of 65 to 67 centemeters and a weight of 260 to 280 grams. It is leather or synthetic leather, with a rubber bladder. For smaller, younger athletes a smaller, lighter ball of the same materials is permissible, as is lowering the height of the net, which is 2.43 meters for the men and 2.24 for women. The net is one meter deep and 9.5 meters long, and should be kept taut, in order that the ball will rebound from it. Two flexible antennae should be fastened to the net above the sidelines, and the ball must cross the net between the antennae.

FIVB World Tour Beach uniform. USA photo courtesy of FIVB

There are only a few major differences between Beach and Indoor Volleyball. The ten meter attack line, beyond which an indoor back row hitter cannot penetrate until after the ball is spiked, is removed on the beach. So is the center line under the net. Athletes can go under the net as long as they do not interfere with the other team. A touch on a blocked ball counts as one of that team's three hits, unlike the indoor game where the team still has three touches. Teams switch ends after every five points. The Beach Volleyball tends to be a little heavier and softer. (Note: the International FIVB pro circuit has adopted a smaller Beach Volleyball court for its two person circuit).

CHAPTER 10

An Overview of Volleyball Injuries and Their Prevention

by Jonathan Reeser, MD PhD, Past FIVB Medical Commission

Volleyball was invented by William Morgan over 100 years ago as a less stressful sporting alternative to basketball for the businessmen who frequented the Springfield, Massachusetts YMCA. Since then, volleyball has grown into one of the most popular participation sports in the world. Although many people unfamiliar with the sport view it as a laid-back form of backyard recreation, in fact volleyball at its highest level has become an explosive sport characterized by skills—such as spiking—that require both athleticism and explosive power. These skills can place tremendous loads upon the musculorskeletal systems of volleyball athletes, thereby putting them at considerable risk of injury.

37th annual Motherlode Tourney
Aspen CO, 600 teams strong.
Photo by John Kessel

Spiking is perhaps the quintessential volleyball skill: leaping high into the air, the athlete reaches out overhead to "attack" the volleyball, sending it past the opponent's block at speeds approaching 110 miles per hour. The spike is thrilling for volleyball fans to watch, but it is perhaps even more thrilling for the volleyball athlete to perform! However, it is also a difficult skill to master, and consequently considerable time is spent by both novice and elite volleyball players alike in spiking practice and in developing the jumping ability that is a critical component of spiking success. It has been estimated that an elite volleyball player, practicing and competing sixteen to twenty hours per week, may perform as many as 40,000 spikes in a season. This volume of spiking places enormous demands on the muscles, tendons, ligaments and bones of the shoulders, knees, ankles, and lower back. It should therefore come as no surprise that these body parts are the most frequently injured among volleyball players.

Ankle sprain injuries are the most common volleyball related injury. The majority of ankle sprains occur when an athlete lands on the foot of a teammate or off an opponent during a "confrontation" between spiker and blockers at the net. Most commonly this scenario results in a lateral ankle sprain, as the ligaments on the outer aspect of the ankle are stretched or torn by the acute overload of the foot turning inward suddenly and unexpectedly.

Fortunately, most ankle sprain injuries are not severe enough to require surgery. However, they should be aggressively rehabilitated. Once injured, the ankle can easily be sprained again. The injured athlete should therefore use an ankle stirrup type brace for at least six months after the injury to minimize the risk of recurrent injury upon return to play. Optimal rehabilitation includes a program of "proprioceptive" exercises to help the athlete regain normal ankle function and neuromuscular control. Such exercises should also be incorporated into an athlete's preseason conditioning program to minimize their risk of ankle sprain injury during the season.

Injuries to the shoulder and knee occur most often as the result of chronic overload. Jumper's knee (also known as patellar tendinopathy) is the most common overuse injury in volleyball. Perhaps the two greatest risk factors for jumper's knee are the volume of jumping/jump training the athlete is asked to perform, and playing on hard, unforgiving surfaces. At least one study has shown that jumper's knee is less common among beach volleyball players than it is among indoor volleyball athletes. Prevention and treatment of jumper's knee consists of strengthening and conditioning the thigh and hip muscles so that they can effectively absorb the shock of landing from jump after jump. Analysis of technique is also important, as bending too deeply at the knees or excessively "toeing in" during the loading and take off phases of the jump can predispose the athlete to jumper's knee as well.

Similarly, the most significant risk factor for shoulder problems among volleyball players is probably the number of spikes attempted during the course of a season. The shoulder is an extremely mobile joint. This mobility, which allows the volleyball athlete to swing high for a spike or reach out for a block, is dependent upon the precise function of the rotator cuff and the muscles that stabilize the scapula (shoulder blade). These muscles must be well conditioned and coordinated to ensure pain-free shoulder function. Through repetition and sheer volume of training, however, the muscles and tendons of the shoulder girdle are frequently overloaded to the point of fatigue, leading to wear and tear and, frequently, to outright injury. Treatment of typical volleyball-related shoulder problems, such as rotator cuff tendinopathy, usually includes restoring normal, pain-free range of motion through flexibility training and restoring normal strength and endurance through a program of exercise/resistance training.

Over the last twenty years, the ability of sports medicine professionals to diagnose and treat athletic injuries has improved dramatically. Athletes are returning from serious injuries faster than ever before due to aggressive rehabilitation programs. Perhaps the greatest remaining challenge in the field of sports medicine is to design and implement programs that will prevent injuries from occurring in the first place. Although injuries cannot be entirely avoided, our present understanding of the basic risk factors associated with the most common volleyball-related injuries can help coaches and athletes prepare themselves and their teams for a successful season with minimal risk of injury. Several strategies that can be adopted in an effort to reduce an athlete's risk of volleyball-related injury are presented below. Although certainly not exhaustive, the principles briefly outlined form the foundation of a sound volleyball injury prevention program.

High School Volleyball. Photo by John Kessel

For additional information the interested reader is referred to the United States Volleyball Association publication entitled *The Complete Guide to Volleyball Conditioning*.

1. **Follow a sport-specific program of strength training and conditioning.**

   Volleyball athletes must maintain good cardiovascular fitness, but must also train to become strong and powerful.Well-conditioned muscles are better able to endure the demands of sport participation, and are less likely to become injured. Fitness also allows the athlete to maintain form and technique throughout a match, further minimizing the risk of fatigue-related injuries. Elite athletes train for volleyball throughout the year, but cycle the intensity and composition of their workouts so that they achieve and maintain peak fitness during the competition season. There is evidence that this practice, known as "periodization," further reduces an athlete's risk of injury.

2. **Avoid overtraining.**

   Adequate rest is almost as important to an athlete's development and performance as proper training. Athletes who train too hard may not give their bodies sufficient time to recover, resulting in an increased risk of overuse injuries. Each athlete has a unique tolerance for training and individual needs for rest and recovery, making it difficult for a coach to take a "cook book" approach to training for all members of the team. Athletes who overtrain without sufficient rest are also at risk for developing a syndrome of mental and physical fatigue commonly referred to as "burnout."

3. **Maintain proper nutrition and hydration.**

   Consuming a balanced diet with adequate caloric intake ensures that the athlete will have sufficient energy stores to allow full participation throughout the season.

Dietary protein intake provides the building blocks to repair injured tissues, while fats and carbohydrates serves as fuel for the athlete's fire. Sufficient fluid intake (preferably water or a sport's drink during competition) prevents dehydration and minimizes the risk of developing heat illness. Coaches should be particularly attentive for recurrent injury among female athletes, as this may indicate the presence of the "female athlete triad," a condition characterized by disordered eating (typically anorexia), which in turn leads to irregular or even absent menstrual cycles (amenorrhea), and eventually to loss of bone mass (osteoporosis).

4. **Avoid early sport and position specialization.**

Volleyball is a sport that can be enjoyed by young and old alike. However, there is evidence that engaging young athletes in overly structured, competitive programs may increase their risk of injury. The American Academy of Pediatrics Committee on Sports Medicine and Fitness has discouraged "specialization in a single sport before adolescence," and it seems reasonable to conclude that the volume of training in developing athletes should be limited in order to reduce the risk of developing overuse injuries. Unfortunately, no studies have been done to quantify what represents an appropriate training load for the young volleyball athlete. Athletes, coaches, and parents must therefore be particularly attentive to the early warning signs of overuse injury, including activity-related pain and deteriorating performance.

5. **Properly rehabilitate existing injuries.**

Research has shown that a body part, once injured, is more likely to be injured again upon returning to play. To prevent acute injuries from becoming chronic injuries, it is imperative that the injured athlete receive careful evaluation from a sports medicine provider, so that an accurate diagnosis can be made and a comprehensive treatment program started. Typically the athlete will be allowed to return to competition once they can perform sport-specific skills, such as jumping and spiking, without pain. However, a truly thorough program will rehabilitate the athlete "beyond the absence of symptoms," thereby having that area of the body to be even stronger than it was before the injury occurred.

This philosophy requires that the athlete's trainer, therapist, or team physician identify and address any structural and/or functional factors that contributed to (or resulted from) the injury. For example, an athlete with a stress fracture of the lower back may have developed inflexibility of the hamstrings and subconsciously altered their spiking form so as to minimize stress on the lower back. Unless these factors are identified and corrected during the rehabilitation process, the athlete may subsequently develop shoulder pain from their altered mechanics.

6. **Practice proper technique.**

As we have seen, most ankle sprains occur when an athlete lands on a teammate's or opponent's foot while making a play at the net. Good blocking footwork and controlled spike jump approaches and landings can minimize the likelihood of contact-related injuries about the centerline.

Fortunately, when compared with other sports, volleyball can be considered a relatively safe sport. The overall rate of injury among participants is lower in volleyball than in sports such as soccer and basketball. The risk of injury in American football, for example, is estimated to be more than five times that of volleyball. Volleyball athletes are predisposed to certain injuries in a pattern that is unique to the demands of the sport. Volleyball is a sport in evolution, particularly over the last several years, as new rules and strategies have been introduced to the game at a rapid rate. The full impact of these changes on volleyball injury patterns will not be appreciated for years to come. It is important that volleyball coaches, parents, and athletes work together with sports medicine professionals to minimize the risk of injury inherent to the sport.

In this manner not only will each participant find the sport enjoyable and rewarding, but they will be permitted to fully develop their athletic potential in the great sport of volleyball.

2009 National State Games Senior Division Champions.
Photo by John Kessel

CHAPTER 11

Why It Is Important to Get Every Member of the Family Involved

by Michael O'Hara

The fact that the volleyball net separates the opposing teams makes the sport both peaceful and classy. At the age of ten and eight, my brother and I learned the basics of the sport in a way that fit both our competitive spirit and pocketbook. We placed a string between the top of a swing and a nearby tree, at a height of about six feet, blew up our most durable balloon and got it on, hour after hour, and day after day. The surface was dirt, and we carried a lot of it into the shower with us every night before dinner, but gosh was it fun. As actor Humphrey Bogart used to say, "it was the beginning of a beautiful friendship."

Vail Father Son twelve and under Division. Photos by John Kessel

It also turned out to be an excellent way to learn body and ball control, and how to look past the balloon in order to see and avoid the block, when spiking. Volleyball is one of the few sports that is great fun to practice. Even the solitary practice of taking a volleyball and passing, serving and spiking against a backboard or wall or garage door can be challenging, especially when there are no pals around to play with. To borrow a famous

saying, "the family that plays together, stays together." I strongly agree that this is an accurate statement. Whether a family goes indoor to play, or the weather is good enough to play on the grass, sand or even pool volleyball, a good time can be had by all. If there are some preteen players, it may be more enjoyable to play on a lowered net, since the equivalent of socking the baseball with the bat, the punch line in volleyball is spiking it! The lower net will afford that opportuni-ty to those shorter play-ers, just jumping up and taking a big swing! These two shots are of the 10th Annual Father Son/Father Daughter Doubles Tournament in Vail, Colorado, actually held on Father's Day Sunday. While all of the volleyball venues are great for family play, the beach game is especially unique. The lifestyle feeling of sheer pleasure in leaping and scrambling in the sand for the ball, finishing the game and then running and diving into the nearby water and repeating the process all day long, is impossible to duplicate.

Two of the royal families of Santa Monica beaches, where volleyball, and its organized counterpart professional volleyball was born, are the Sato's (whose most famous son is Gary) and the Smith's (whose most famous son is Sinjin). Both of those families are shining examples as they continue to play family Beach Volleyball together and thrive. Every summer the Sato's hosted a beach party for their many pals at Will Rogers State Beach and they place several volleyball nets at right angles together, creating three contiguous courts, with each of three teams defending a court and being able to spike into either of the two other courts. Sensational fun!! As with the other versions of volleyball, and with most sports, the ability to control the ball remains the essential factor of success.

The joy involved in all of these different disciplines, with family members or neighborhood friends, is what makes volleyball the wonderful, versatile sport that it is.

Karch Kiraly, three-time Olympic Gold medalist and current assistant National Women's Team coach delivers a family skill Clinic to 500 kids and parents in 2010. Photo by John Kessel

CHAPTER 12

Hollywood Moguls Develop the International Volleyball Association (IVA)

by Michael O'Hara

I had the negative experience of recently attending the services of David Wolper, creator of the unbelievably successful documentary series called Roots, that was ranked in several ways as the number one of all time, aesthetically as well as financially. The funeral was in August, 2010.

I have attended every Summer Olympic Games since the first Games for the sport of volleyball in Tokyo, 1964. I first met David Wolper, when my old friend Bud Greenspan introduced him to me at the 1972 Games in Munich, where David was producing his documentary on those Games, called "Visions of Eight." I was delighted that a film maker of his immense talent and skill was that interested in sport, and his film turned out to be superb. Several months after the Olympics ended, he called me and requested a meeting. I learned that David had invited some his close pals to come as his guest to the Munich Olympic Games, contribute ideas to his film, and enjoy a pass to any event that they wanted to choose. To make a long story short, they all fell in love with Indoor Volleyball, and were now committed to "produce" the professional sport of volleyball on the west coast! Since by that time I had helped found leagues concerning professional basketball, hockey and Track and Field, they invited basketballer Wilt Chamberlain and I to join their group. Wilt had discovered Beach Volleyball late in his basketball career, but learned extremely fast, and truly loved both the game and the relaxed, beachy atmosphere.

Their group was comprised of the "who's who" of show biz! Starting from right to left below are David Gerber and Martin Starger, producers of many successful detective television series, Berry Gordy, owner of Motown Records, Barry Diller, at that time President of Fox Studios, Wolper, Chamberlain, my terrific attorney of three other leagues, Don Regan, movie producer Jerry Leider, and myself.

This was the greatest assembly of talent and financial power that I had ever been associated with, and it was very exciting to be able to inform them of ways to keep their financial budgets "skinny," while providing terrific entertainment. In fact, we needed an additional owner for San Jose, and I invited my travel company president for the other three leagues, to sit in on our owners meeting, since he had graduated from San Jose State. After the meeting, our League President David Wolper and I took Peter V. Ueberroth aside and invited him to join our owners group. Pete quickly said "NO," and David asked why. His response was, "because all of you giants of your profession are talking about spending dollars when you should be talking about spending dimes!" Volleyball is not football, baseball or basketball, and should not be treated that way. (Note: about a decade later Pete became the President of the Los Angeles Olympic Organizing Committee, and proved his thesis on spending dimes not dollars, realizing a quarter of a billion dollars "surplus" while putting on a terrific 1984 Olympic Games).

Every one of the IVA owners absorbed the message, and the league made great strides, losing less than $100,000 per franchise in either of the first two years, and securing good attendance numbers and television ratings. Then David's health failed, and his doctor told him if he wanted to live more than a year or two longer he should retire from his main business and all of his side businesses. I was appointed IVA Commissioner replacing David Wolper (now deceased) and quickly sold my Santa Barbara Prefessional Volleyball Club ownership. The minute he walked out our league door, all of his pals said, we too have had fun, but are going to follow David on to more adventures in the motion picture business.

I quickly moved from owner to League Commissioner, but the new owners of the clubs we motivated to join us were less skilled and financially secure, so after four more years, the IVA ceased to operate, and most of the male and female players moved with me that next summer over to the Fabulous Forum in Inglewood, California, which had very little business in the summer time. NBA Lakers owner Jerry Buss and I became the equity owners of Team Cup Volleyball. That chapter in the evolution of the sport of volleyball is described in the next chapter.

Meanwhile, the USAV has been carefully building a strong and motivated management team to grow the grass roots groups of junior and adult females and males to join their appropriate Indoor and Beach volleyball organizations. As the Demographics 1980 to 2009 membership growth chart at the chapter 1 indicates, these groups have grown from 5,000 members in 1980 to 248,000 in 2009. To enjoy such excellent growth, that has not been deterred by the recession brewing over the last two and one half years, is proof that the grass roots approach is indeed effective, when the right management is hired and extremely motivated.

Most importantly, this kind of growth is being repeated in most of the 219 other National Governing Bodies (NGB's) around the world, and the FIVB is supporting that grass roots effort with their strong leadership and financial position. As stated earlier, while the sport of soccer enjoys the organization and support of 204 NGB's worldwide, and basketball has 216 NGB's, volleyball has the premier position of having the most National Governing Bodies of 220, and growing! Those countries NGB's, and the unique pace at which they have also grown, and will continue to multiply, represent the core strength of the sport of volleyball.

Polish star Stan Gosciniak played in IVA for the Santa Barbara Spikers, owned by Michael O' Hara.

Ed Skorek, star of the Polish National volleyball team that upset highly favored Russia to win the God medal in the Montreal, 1976 Olympics. It was the only Gold medal won by Poland. Michael O'Hara Commissioner of IVA on right.

CHAPTER 13

Team Cup Volleyball

by Michael O'Hara

For six years, starting in August of 1987, I partnered with Los Angeles Lakers owner Jerry Buss concerning a summer event for an excellent stadium he owned in Inglewood, California, called the Great Western Forum. His initial proposal to me was to hold track meets every week, with the professional international stars that I had signed up immediately following the Munich Olympics.

I indicated that I had found that such a track meet drew excellent crowds the first night, but not at all well in the same city thereafter until the following year. I then told him of my concept of Team Cup Volleyball. The fact that we were able to attract some of the world's finest men and women volleyball players from both the indoor game and the beach game, enabled us to secure a terrific television company, Prime Ticket, along with some fine sponsors for each of the four teams. Since the "Mother's Milk" of any professional sporting venture is television and sponsorship, this launched our concept into business.

Jerry's daughter Jeanie soon married one of our star Olympic players, Steve Timmons, and joined us in producing the league competitions. Jeanie was especially productive to our cause when she was able to persuade her husband's Italian professional team to come and play in our Team Cup competition for the league's final season four years later.

We had the enthusiastic support of most of the players. However, our television broadcaster, Prime Ticket, was even more impressed with the product that we presented to the sporting public. They already greatly appreciated the fact that the court size fit perfectly into the lens of their cameras. They also like the fact that the volleyball, composed of blue, white and yellow coloring was so much more distinct for both television and live event spectators, in addition to being larger than the tennis ball, baseball, and golf ball.

From left to right, Linesman Ryan O'Hara, Setter Gary Sato, and Spiker Tim Hovland.

OFFICIAL PROGRAM OF THE INTERNATIONAL VOLLEYBALL ASSOCIATION

Their only concern was that, in the past, using "side out scoring" a volleyball game could last only ten minutes, or as long as one hour, to complete. If it was too fast, they had the problem of not getting all their commercials played. If it ran too long, it injured their relationship with those sponsors of the next program that did not get their full allotment of commercials played.

When we presented our matches, with "point per serve" scoring, (to twenty-five points instead of fifteen) those matches never ran too late, or finished too early. (Note: making your television partner happy is really a worthwhile objective).

I collected the comparison television tapes, plus letters from both television and the players and headed to Lausanne, Switzerland, Headquarters of the FIVB, to their year end annual meeting of the Rules Committee. My presentation was one of forty-two submissions for rule changes, coming in from around the world.

After long testing and deliberation, I was informed that this rule was one of two to be held over for additional testing! After many more long test sessions, the FIVB Rules Committee changed the name to a better one, "RALLY SCORING SYSTEM."

After about three more years, I was part of a small committee that attended a men's tournament in Tokyo and a women's tournament in Seoul, testing two different versions of my rule, and then we had a final long session of negotiating, and finally, The VOTE!. The majority vote came in to try it for the fifth game of any match only!

Another two years went by before the '96 Atlanta Olympics Indoor Volleyball was played. The Men's Volleyball Finals was a masterpiece, but lasted over three hours! By the time the final game was played, the initially full house had melted down to attendance of less than 50% full. Both Head Coaches immediately wrote to the FIVB Rules Committee and requested that the Rally Scoring System be used for every game. The change became effective relatively quickly!

CHAPTER 14

FIVB International Women's Beach Volleyball Championship in Hong Kong

by Michael O'Hara

In mid-1983, I was asked by President Peter Ueberroth to leave the sports division of the LAOOC, where the twenty-eight commissioners I had hired and trained were ready and I became Vice President, Television and Communication, in order to sell our '84 Olympic television rights to 152 foreign countries. One of the earliest negotiations was with Clarence Chang, who represented a group that consisted of Hong Kong, Taiwan and Korea. I was very impressed with the firm but the classy way he negotiated with me, and my part time lawyer/senior partner for Latham & Watkins, Barry Sanders.

Clarence Chang and Michael O'Hara at the Beijing 2008 Olympic Games

Clarence Chang is my long time Olympic friend, and we are currently working on an effective way to translate this international publication into Mandarin, so the last quarter of the world's population can join with us to place the sport of volleyball where it richly deserves to be.

He also amazed me during the Olympic Games period, when he did a superb job of preparing for each of the countries, plus China, a two hour program that featured the medal winning players for that specific country, in the appropriate language. The complete enjoyment of the Games is predicated upon nationalism, so every nation roots with great passion for their male or female contestants. Thus, when their athlete wins an Olympic medal, every man, woman, and child in that country goes bonkers!

Clarence and I became close friends, and decided to produce the first FIVB Women's Beach Doubles Championship in Hong Kong.

The competition presented the week of August 19, 2001, was a success. We had the enthusiastic support of the Hong Kong Volleyball Federation (NGB). We rented Victoria Park, the leading tennis center in Hong Kong, had twenty-two tons of manufactured sand, of special texture for the athletes, and color for the television company, barged in and deposited upon the six terrific tennis courts, and the playing facilities were impeccable.

The first day, we had a good crowd, but our questionnaire at the match revealed that many of the women spectators did not like to be in the sun for long periods, so we immediately rescheduled our future matches to the evening, and strongly advertised the fact. Also, the banking corporation that had indicated that they wanted to be our Title Sponsor, made a last minute decision to decline the honor, so we had to quickly move to the next highest bidder, which was one tenth of the amount that we had been asking. The tournament was well received, by the public and the television and newspaper media, with the Brazilian National Team winning the Gold, the United States featuring young Misty May and Kerry Walsh receiving the Silver, and China taking the Bronze.

However, two weeks later the disaster in New York City, with the dual bombing of our Twin Towers, called "9/11," occurred! Suddenly, the number of international flights were greatly reduced, and almost all of the planned international sports events were cancelled or postponed!

Needless to say, both of the above mentioned disappointments caused our Hong Kong financial backers to hold off on planning a future annual FIVB Beach Volleyball Tournament.

Clarence Chang is my long time Olympic friend, and we are currently working on an effective way to translate this international publication into Mandarin, so the last quarter of the world's population can join with us to place the sport of Volleyball where it richly deserves to be.

A pre-tournament sports conference six weeks before the athletes arrived, featuring winners of the Miss Hong Kong Beauty Contest, along with tournament chairman Michael O'Hara.

(CHAPTER 15)

The Contribution of Wallyball to the Sport of Volleyball

by Michael O'Hara

While this book has illuminated many different variations of volleyball, there is one that has not as yet been mentioned. It is over three decades old and at its peak, had about 800,000 male and female players in the United States. That sport is Wallyball, and it is most popular in areas of the country where the weather is not good during the winter months for playing outside, like Chicago, Detroit, and New York.

The only father and son presidential team in American history, George H. and George W. Bush, played Wallyball powerfully and extremely well. They used to play at their presidential retreat, Camp David, when many of their younger visitors would wind up going into their racquetball court where a volleyball net has been stretched across the center of the court, and playing Wallyball. That group includes superb athletes like Montreal Olympic Decathlon Gold medalist Bruce Jenner and weightlifting champion/actor turned Govenor Arnold Swartzenegger.

The court size is smaller, about the size of the new Beach Volleyball court, which is about one third smaller then the indoor volleyball configuration. Teams of two, three or four can play, serving or spiking the ball directly over the net or off one of the side walls. Since the ability to pass or dig the ball off the wall is an acquired skill, the Bush team had the advantage of having already flattened the learning curve. Wallyball is a very social game, with almost 50% of the players being female. It is also a better aerobic workout then Indoor Volleyball for several reasons: when the ball is shanked off the arms and hits the wall it is still in play, and when it finally touches the ground it cannot roll elsewhere and so the next play can commence immediately.

A major contribution to the sport of volleyball was made at its inception. Co-founder-owner of Wallyball Michael O'Hara conceived a rally scoring system whereby each time a ball is served, a point is made by the rally winning team, eliminating the "side out" whereby only the serving team could make a point (which tends to be like kissing your sister). The need in Wallyball for such a rule was due to the necessity for Wallyball players to use the racquetball court for a limited, specific time, (like an hour or two), and then have to relinquish it back to the racquetball players.

Joe Garcia (Left) and Michael O'Hara (Right),
Founders of Wallyball, with Olympian and sports television broadcaster
Paul Sunderland

In '88, when O'Hara teamed up with L.A. Lakers owner Jerry Buss to create a professional volleyball league called Team Cup Volleyball, he included the rule and it became a favorite of not only the pro players of both sexes, but of more

One of thirty annual Wallyball National Championships held in cities like New York, Chicago, Los Angeles, Detroit, Phoenix, etc.

audience as well. The broadcaster especially love the fact that the matches no longer finished too soon, thereby eliminating the opportunity to play all of the sponsors, commercials or, worse yet, lasted too long, so that their next program would be held up.

George Cassius, our Executive Director of Wallyball International, Inc., with and active male and female American population of 800,000 at the peak of its popularity to organize terrific regional tournaments, and collage competitions out of his New York City headquarters.

The rally scoring system became a temporary part of the international Beach Volleyball program on January 1, 2001, and has since become an important and permanent fixture for every part of volleyball, including the Olympic Games.

& WORLD REPORT

U.S.News

DECEMBER 6, 1999   www.usnews.com

Camp David is a slam-dunk

Nothing has been dissed by the first family more than Camp David, the presidential weekend mountain retreat the Clintons have reserved mostly for holidays like Thanksgiving and for soul-baring Cabinet retreats. But no matter which of the current front-runners wins the White House, that's going to change. Aides to **Al Gore** and **George W. Bush** say they're both drooling over the chance of seeing their nameplate on a Camp David golf cart. "It's a dream," says a Bushie. The Texas governor has a real thing for the rustic retreat, having spent many a weekend in its log cabins when Dad was prez. Should he perform as predicted and waltz into the Oval Office, the Navy and Marine unit that runs the camp had better dig out the Wallyball net. Camp David playmates of Bush recall how the prez and his son used to enlist civilian and military aides to play their favorite game—a combination of volleyball and racquetball. "Junior used to spike like crazy. He'd hit you in the head," says one. "It will be back."

(CHAPTER 16)

Volleyball Guidelines for Parents, Referees, Volunteers and Fans

by John Kessel, USA Volleyball

In order to keep our sport growing, parents are clearly the key connection to insure that kids are having a positive experience in playing volleyball. Communication is vital, with the roles of each area defined. A mandatory parent meeting is part of this network that will help everyone maximize their investment of time . . . When choosing a program, at any level, parents should know the following things:

PROGRAM REQUIREMENTS

Grade point average
Practice participation
Tournament participation
Fundraising activities
Officiating duties
Time commitment
Uniforms
Travel expectations—local or out of town
Insurance information

FORMS

Program membership
Player questionnaire
Medical history and Consent

Parent / volunteer information form
Telephone contact tree

The parent at the youth level especially is often needed as a coach. When the program does not need you as a coach, your assistance is still valuable in filling the following roles:

Securing playing/practice facilities
Additional player recruitment
Additional coaching recruitment
Hosting of out of town teams
Travel and chaperone assistance
Team organizational, season planning, evaluation meeting
  attendance
Fundraising planning and coordination
Car pooling
Practice attendance and observation
Timely payment of fees or dues

Tips for Being a Great Spectator

Far more than the winning and losing are the lessons learned in the process of tournament play. To quote Socrates, "I believe that we cannot live better than in seeking to become still better than we are." The sport of volleyball is unique in its core cooperative nature and its strength in building character. The ability to cooperate is far more important to human survival than the ability to compete. Success is a journey, not a destination. "Winning and losing are temporary, but friendships last forever," is a Chinese proverb of great truth. We ask that your role from the sidelines and stands match that which we are developing through top coaching education programs and training.

Tip No. 1: Keep POSITIVE support, encouragement, cheerleading, and general hollering and yelling to a MAXIMUM on the sidelines.

When players are working hard, they need and deserve everyone's best POSITIVE encouragement and support. They need to know you are there. Most teams have a tough enough time developing a sense of teamwork and achievement as they are also developing their own individual experience and skill. They DO NOT need to hear YOUR anxiety piled on top of their own when the game is going poorly.

Tip No. 2: Just one word on criticizing either players, coaches or referees: DON'T.

Publicly criticizing players on your team can really hurt morale. They will already have an excellent idea, from all the practicing they have already done, about their errors. They do NOT need reminders from their families, friends and other spectators. The players for the other team are also doing their best and in truth are probably no more aggressive than the players on your team. Criticism is simply poor sportsmanship and leads to unnecessary bad feelings on and off the playing area. The unfortunate spectacle of a supposed adult shouting insults at a child or other adult is disgusting. Volleyball is a game, not a war. When the opponents make a great play, give them positive encouragement too.

The referees are making judgment calls on each and every contact, and will err at times, though far fewer than the best player on the team you are cheering for. Referees may make mistakes, but they never make a bad call in their heart. The referee might ignore you, but also has the right to ask you to leave the playing area. Either situation is at best distracting from the most important thing going on, the player's competition.

Tip No. 3: Leave the coaching of the player to the staff.

This is a game for the players. Coaches are already there on the bench to guide the players and in the stress of the game, there needs to be just one source of feedback, the coach's. If you think an athlete is not doing what should be done, tell the coaches in private, not the player. As others not on the team occasionally discover, a player may be doing exactly what the coaches have instructed. Either way, a parent can help a player's development much better working with the coaches, not independently. One more thing, no calling out "Point! Point!" from the stands. The coaching staff and even the referees know a point has been scored. You might, however, help take game statistics and scout from that vantage point.

Tip No. 4: Set an example in your actions and words.

Do not break the rules of the tournament, by sneaking in, leaving a mess, smoking, or drinking any substance where it is not permitted. Players on the court can be removed from the game for foul language, and spectators can too. Degrading actions and words are the bane of sports character development. Leave the gym in better shape than you found it in, physically and verbally, by being a great role model.

Tip No. 5: Remember, it is a GAME.

Therefore, it is supposed to be FUN. Please remember, YOUR attitude in the spectating area can affect the mood and success of the team. Any spectator who persists in inappropriate behavior may be asked to leave the gym. Emotions run high in competition, and feelings are easily hurt. Be tolerant. The place to talk about the game with the coaches is not in the gym, and not around the players. The program these young athletes are part of is USA Volleyball's JUNIOR OLYMPIC Volleyball programming. Take a moment to read the Olympic Creed and the Oath of Athletes:

The most important thing in the Olympic Games is not to win but to take part, just as the most important thing in life is not the triumph but the struggle. The essential thing is not to have conquered but to have fought well.

In the name of all competitors, I promise that we will take part in these Olympic Games, respecting and abiding by all the rules which govern them in the true spirit of sportsmanship, for the glory of sport and the honor of our teams.

—Baron Pierre de Coubertin

Girls Junior. Olympic Club volleyball. Photo by John Kessel

Tips for the Parents of Prospective College Hopefuls

A. Talk to your athletic son/daughter and find out what schools they are interested in. Have them contact these schools by the end of their junior year or the beginning of their senior year in high school.

1. Have them provide the college with complete and accurate information:
    a. Height and weight.
    b. Position they play and specialties.
    c. Club name and high school they attend.
    d. Vertical reach, blocking reach, spiking reach.
    e. Volleyball honors.
    f. Class rank and grade point average.
    g. ACT and/of/SAT scores and academic interest.
    h. Additional information such as:

        1. Right or left handedness.
        2. Club and team honors.
        3. Newspaper articles.
        4. Other sports honors.
        5. Video tape of them if available.
        6. References (club and high school coaches names, addresses, and phone numbers).
        7. A schedule of their high school or club matches.
        8. Tell the coach their strengths.

    i. Have them ask for academic information. Make sure that your athlete knows that the educational program of the school is more important in the long run than the quality of their volleyball program. Tell them to select a school and not a coach because there is no guarantee that the coach will be there for the athlete's entire volleyball career.

2. Learn the recruiting rules of the various collegiate governing bodies such as the NCAA, NAIA, NJCAA. Some conferences have restrictions that apply only to their member institutions. It is important for you to protect the interested player. The player cannot afford to jeopardize their career by not knowing the regulations.

3. Learn the recruiting and eligibility rules of the State College Association. Each state has its own rules. Make sure that your athlete knows and follows all the recruiting rules.

4. Have your athlete look at a number of schools. Remember that recruiting is a two-year process. Even though your athlete may want to attend a certain school, that school may feel that your athlete won't fit into their program. Make sure your athlete is told that it isn't reflective on their skills.

5. Learn or develop a resource on schools' volleyball programs and their academic reputations. Make this information or resource available to your athlete in the recruiting process. USE THE INTERNET!

6. Make sure that your athlete learns about the financial aid programs made available by the schools. Not all schools offer the same types or number of scholarships. Remind them that less than 50% of all college athletes are on any type of scholarship.

7. Help the athlete set and evaluate their priorities in selecting schools. Give the athlete some guidance as to what level of program would be best for them, based on your experience. It is real hard for some athletes to go to programs where they will be sitting on the bench for a year or two especially when they could have gone somewhere else and started as a freshman.

8. Help the athlete prepare physically and mentally. It is obvious that they can't do anything about their height, but they can control their weight, mental attitude and general physical condition. Some colleges have extremely demanding programs that require year-round commitment. Is your student/athlete ready to handle (physically and mentally) this type of program?

9. Talk to the athlete about "senioritis." Make sure they understand education and volleyball are both hard work. Anything you can do to enhance the qualities that

a college coach is looking for in a player (while being honest) will benefit your athlete and your program. College coaches generally look for players who are:

a. Lean (not skinny, but have a body fat count of 15% or less).
b. Physically strong.
c. Well conditioned (stamina).
d. Intelligent.
e. Court aware.
f. Team players (supportive of others).
h. Coachable (capable of incorporating suggestions into actions; listening and respecting the coach and other players).

Refereeing

One of the other fun ways to get involved in the sport is as an official. The same grassroots to Olympic/Paralympic pipeline exists for both referees and scorekeepers. Former Junior Olympic players and parents have gone from just wanting to learn what a referee does, or helping their junior club as a team official—all the way to international travel and competition at World Championships and other elite events. Each of the USA Volleyball regions trains officials, and kids and adults can become rated from a provisional level to that of a National official. Generally, a part day USAV clinic includes:

1. Educational clinic—usually three-four hours in length about all aspects, hand signals, casebook examples and key rule discussions.
2. Test—open book but you must get 100%.
3. Rating session(s)—being observed, taught, and graded after refereeing a scrimmage or, at the higher levels, actual matches.

Officiating payment ranges from nothing, to about $50 for a high school match, and about $100 for a collegiate match, and in some of the higher levels, your travel expenses are also covered. There are national training camps and ratings for Beach Volleyball as well, conducted in a similar fashion to the indoor program. Also, volleyball camps for officials exist, usually utilizing college campuses and refereeing college teams.

The National Federation of State High School Association conducts similar officiating programs for those wanting to referee at the high school level for interscholastic matches. The NCAA, NAIA and other collegiate governing bodies also have a similar officiating training program.

Player Referee.
Photo by John Kessel

For more information, contact your local USA Volleyball Regional Volleyball Association Officiating Coordinator, or the Professional Association of Volleyball Officials (PAVO) at P. O. Box 8660 Topeka, KS 66608 (888) 791-2074 or www.pavo.org

Volunteering

There are dozens of organizations where your volunteer support would be a great help in growing the game and enhancing your appreciation and understanding of the sport. These include the YMCA, YWCA, Boys & Girls Clubs, Police Athletic League, Starlings USA, AAU. At the Regional level of USA Volleyball, leadership positions exist in all areas of the game, including coaching education, team representation, officiating coordination, tournament hosting, disabled programs, board of directors work, public relations, finances and much more.

Disabled Programs

Most people associate disabled sports with the Special Olympics. That world-wide program is the guiding organization for volleyball athletes with mental disabilities, but is only one of seven organizations recognized by the USOC in support of the disabled. Additional volleyball opportunities exist for the deaf, amputee, wheelchair, and other physically disabled athletes. The Paralympic programs combined support approximately 20,000 elite disabled athletes (not including the 438,000 SOI athletes and recreational participants). Currently, there are twenty-five Paralympic Sports, nineteen Summer and six Winter Sports. The best source for US Paralympic information is at www.usparalympics.org.

In October of 1998, U.S. House and Senate amended and renamed the Amateur Sports Act, to the current Olympic and Amateur Sports Act. This Olympic and Amateur Sports Act now fully incorporates Paralympics, clearly reflecting equal status for disabled athletes. It continues the original focus of the Act to integrate disabled sports with non-disabled National Governing Bodies (NGBs). Under the measure the US Paralympics is officially recognized as the national United States Paralympic Committee. A 1994 U.S. Census report showed that 21% of the population was disabled, a percentage certain to grow as the baby boomer population ages.

The USA Women's Sitting Team celebrates their Bronze medal in the 2004 Paralympics. Photo by John Kessel

Discover U.S. Paralympics Online

Visit our Web site to
find Paralympic sport programs in your community,
tell us about Paralympic athletes you know,
apply for a Military Sports Camp
or an Academy Program,
be inspired by incredible Paralympians,
read the latest Paralympic news
and much more!

www.usparalympics.org

Paralympic Sports by Physical Disability Group

Summer Sports	Amputee/ Les Autres	Blind/ Visually Impaired	Spinal Cord Injury	Traumatic Brain Cerebral Palsy/
Archery	✓		✓	✓
Basketball	✓		✓	
Boccia				✓
Cycling	✓	✓	✓	✓
Equestrian	✓	✓	✓	✓
Fencing	✓		✓	✓
Goalball		✓		
Judo		✓		
Powerlifting	✓		✓	✓
Rowing	✓	✓	✓	✓
Rugby			✓	
Sailing	✓	✓	✓	✓
Shooting	✓		✓	✓
Soccer				✓
Swimming	✓	✓	✓	✓
Table Tennis	✓		✓	✓
Tennis	✓		✓	
Track and Field	✓	✓	✓	✓
Volleyball	✓			
Winter Sports				
Alpine Skiing	✓	✓	✓	✓

Disabled Sports Organizations

There are seven Disabled Sports Organizations (DSOs) recognized as US Paralympic member organizations, of which five conduct volleyball programming. www.usparalympics.org for more information on all these groups.

1. Disabled Sports USA (DSUSA)
2. Wheelchair Sport USA (WSUSA)
3. Special Olympics International (SOI)
4. USA Deaf Sports Federation (USADSF)
5. United States Association of Blind Athletes (USABA)
6. Dwarf Athletic Association of America (DAAA)
7. United States Cerebral Palsy Athletic Association (USCPAA)

Here you can see adults playing sitting and kids playing the sitting game over a rope, with three courts of six meters wide by five meters deep fitting onto one regulation court. It is a great warm up game, using people in chairs to be the "standards" at each end.

Photos by John Kessel

Special Olympics International (SOI)

SOI was founded in 1968 by Eunice Kennedy Shiver, and now has chapters in 140 nations, including every state in the USA. The Special Olympics runs on the belief that people with mental disability can, with proper encouragement, learn, enjoy and become physically fit by participating in sports. The Special Olympic World Games is competition for people with cognitive disabilities and is a participatory event where everyone is a winner. Volleyball exists in two forms, regular, where all six players are disabled, and unified, where half the players on the court are able bodied.

Note: Special Olympics International, in conjunction with the USOC, has assumed the responsibility for INAS-FMH athletes in the United States.

Special Olympics International
1325 G. Street, NW #500
Washington, DC 20005-4709
Ph: 202-628-3630
Fax: 202-824-0200
specialolympics@msn.com
www.specialolympics.org

USA Deaf Sports Federation

USADSF (formerly the AAAD—American Association for Athletes of the Deaf) was formed in 1945 to provide regional and national level competition for the deaf. The USA Deaf Volleyball Association (USADVA) is a volunteer organization that serves a dedicated membership consisting of recreational and competitive volleyball players who are deaf and hearing impaired athletes. USADSF joined the World Deaf Organization in 1957, sending the first officially sponsored team to the World Deaf Games. The USADSF is a Non-

Paralympic DSO, and supports approximately 1,800 athletes.

The Deaflympics is a quadrennial international event for deaf and hard of hearing athletes from different countries around the world. The first time an American delegation participated in the Deaf World Games was in 1935 in London, England with only two athletes. In 1969, volleyball was added to the program.

For the past decades, DSFUSA has been preparing and promoting the USA Deaf Men's and Women's Volleyball Teams for international competition. Across the USA, any deaf and hard of hearing volleyball player with fifty-five decibels or higher hearing loss in the better ear (a standard established by the Comités International des Sports des Sourds [CISS]) eligible for tryouts and potential placement on the national deaf volleyball teams. There are both beach doubles and indoor teams for men and women. The beach men have won Silver medals and the USA women's indoor team has won Silver as well in the 2005 and 2009 Deaflympics

Volleyball is one of the most popular sports for the deaf in school, and deaf players can easily compete with the non-deaf on any team. If you are have a hearing impaired athlete, let them know of the opportunities in volleyball, for both boys and girls, where they can play. At the same time, in part due to the non-contact nature of the game, athletes with various levels of disabilities can participate on teams of able bodied teammates. http://www.usdeafsports.org/

USA Deaf Sports Federation
PO Box 910338
Lexington, KY 40591-0338

TTY:	(605) 367-5761
Voice:	(605) 367-5760
Fax:	(605) 782-8441
E-mail:	John J. Knetzger [knetzger@usdeafsports.org]

PARENT CERTIFICATION EXAM

With thanks to recreational sport softball internet newsgroup and the Great Lakes USA Volleyball Region.

I am just glad my kid isn't a setter, as it has probably saved my nervous system over the years. Gone are the days of "having" to make some comment about every little stupid thing. Nowadays I enjoy watching, and cheering any great effort by any kid on the court, on our team or another!

How about Parent Certification, based on these Levels?

LEVEL I: Rec Ball Parent

Out of control, whole life hinges on every set of the game. Referees are blind and you are not sure if the coach might not also need a vision test. Can only leave the gym for a smoke, even though you do not smoke.

LEVEL 2: First Year Traveling Parent

Still reasonably out of control, has no clue to level of play. Thinks their kid is God's Gift, even though she/he sits on the bench all of the time. Life still hinges on every set. Plan every tournament after consulting General Patton's Diaries. Have considered reading the rulebook for more options to contribute from the bleachers.

LEVEL 3: Minimum Two Years Travel Ball Experience Required

Has started to settle down. Understands the game a little better, may even start trusting the coach's ability. Kid is playing more often, so life hinges on games in matches.
Referees seem to be understanding the rules better too.

LEVEL 4: Minimum Four Years Travel Ball Experience

Understands the game. Walks around eating seeds all day and is an expert in snack bar cuisine. Life hinges on whether or not they get in 7:00 morning pool play or the 3:00 afternoon pool so they might get to sleep in and recover from hall patrol. Does not care if the referees show up, as long as the game is played.

LEVEL 5: More Than Five Years Experience

Parent becomes comatose during games, has no clue if their kid is even playing. Hears about a spike she/he buried yesterday. Daydreams about what life would be like if you could have all the money you ever spent on volleyball. Looks forward to the college program picking up the tab for the next four years. Have considered refereeing since they must get paid big dollars to put up with the parents.

CHAPTER 17

The Opportunity to "Pay My Dues" as a Sports Entrepreneur Has Paid Off For the Sport of International Volleyball

By Michael O'Hara

This chapter is a pictorial recording of some of the thirty-six new sports ventures that O'Hara Enterprises International, Inc. (OEI) has undertaken over the last four decades. Some have turned out to be "home runs" and some were "strike outs," and everything in between. However, all prepared me, as valuable experiences, for the next start up challenge. For instance, the

After being promised a noon run through Santa Monica, instead I wound up up dueling with a drunken bar guy, (who coveted my burning torch), in San Pedro at midnight. (I won the duel, by waving said torch in his face).

hiring of one superstar athlete per team worked so well for the American Basketball Association, that we immediately made that a requirement for the opening year for the World Hockey Association, starting with hockey superstar Bobby Hull.

In the early 1970's, OEI had two sports starting up at the same time: The International Track Association and The International Volleyball Association. During that period, we had ninety-five employees on the payroll, mainly athletes, and the rest were managers of world class international track athletes and world class volleyball players for a Santa Barbara franchise.

Another four year, 24/7 commitment to the LA Olympic Organizing Committee of the 1984 Olympic Games caused us to use all that we had learned from previous sports management experiences in order to put on a terrific Olympic Games.

Michael O'Hara with Mixed Beach Tournament partner Edie Conrad.

Michael O'Hara 1984 Olympic Press Conference

Michael O'Hara interviewing Peter V. Ueberroth, President LAOOC in
Moscow Spartakiade 1979, one year before Moscow 1980 Olympics (which
were later boycotted).

Michael O'Hara's induction into the Volleyball Hall of Fame.

Michael O'Hara's induction into the Beach Volleyball Hall of Fame (Florida).

1984 press conference announcing the sale of TV rights to Rupert
Murdoch's Channel 10 Australia.
(left to right) Michael O'Hara, International Olympic Committee Secretary
General Madame Monique Berloux, President of LAOOC Peter Uberroth
and Channel 10 Managing Director Wilf Barker.

As an honored guest of Rupert Murdoch, owner of the 1984 Olympics for Australia's Channel 10, Michael O'Hara played a "mean" game of tennis with the world's number one professional, John Newcomb, in January 1984.

Michael O'Hara at the Salt Lake City Winter Olympic Games, with Olympic Gold medal French skier Jean Claude Killey. O'Hara has attended every Summer Olympic Games since he played in Tokyo, 1964. He was also playing various meaningful roles at the Winter Games in Calgary, 1988.

(right to left) Michael O'Hara, Mike Bright, Miss California Marylyn Tindall, Gene Selznick, Ron Lang. The top two volleyball teams in the world in the early 1960s.

VOLLEYBALL

MANHATTAN BEACH OPEN

Battle isn't legendary

I am writing to comment on the "Battle of the Century" article by Jon Hastings. It was a very nice idea to bring these legends back into the public eye but I feel compelled to clear up some inaccuracies.

Since the late 1950's the Off Shore Manhattan Beach Open has been widely regarded as one of the world's most competitive and prestigious pro beach volleyball tournaments. Hailed as "the Wimbledon of the sand," "the granddaddy of them all" and "the players favorite," this event historically has more teams than any professional beach volleyball tournament in the world. While other tournaments have 36 teams or less, this year's Off Shore Manhattan Beach Open will draw 64 teams including a large number of local qualifiers who participate at the nonprofessional level.

The crowds are equally as robust. Last year, Off Shore and the Association of Volleyball Professionals produced a tournament which attracted the largest crowd in beach volleyball history — more than 50,000 people attended throughout the weekend. This year fans will come for three days to watch the many teams battle for $75,000 in prize money on the 16-court layout.

Besides the sheer magnitude of the tournament and its spectators, the Off Shore Manhattan Beach Open is rich in history and tradition. In the earlier days of volleyball, if Manhattan was the only event a player won, he considered the summer a success.

Only six players have ever won five Manhattan Opens: the team of Mike O'Hara and Mike Bright during the sixties; Ron Von Hagen in the late sixties and early seventies; Jim Menges in the late seventies and early eighties and the team of Tim Hovland and Mike Dodd throughout

the eighties. This year both Tim H... Mike Dodd, now teamed with differe... have the opportunity to take the all-ti... six wins.

Players savor a win at the Off Sh... tan Beach Open because of its rich t... also because it's a difficult compet... Manhattan Beach has especially... which makes it difficult for players t... move quickly. Because of its dark... large amount of iron, the sand heats... than most beaches. Couple that wit... rally through the large tournament d... have an exhausting, exhilarating tou...

For the second year in a row, Off... title sponsor of the renowned tourn... Tim Hovland, who represents Off S... AVP tour, is looking to set a record w... Manhattan Open title.

"In 1982, the first time we won the... Beach Open we came out of the los... to one of the sweetest wins and... days of my life," he recalls. "Rig... tournament I went into full body cram... days no one knew what to do, so... threw me in the back of his pickup a... home to celebrate all evening. We're... sophisticated today, but one thing... the same —everyone wants to win N...

If there's a tournament that play... there's a tournament not to be mis... 32nd annual Off Shore Manhattan B... Be there July 5-7 for the finest in p... men's beach volleyball.

• Ron Von Hagen and Ron Lang seeded No. 10. Give me a break and please get a clue. I was able to watch and play beach volleyball from the early '60s to the present. I have never seen a better team than Lang and Von Hagen. Ron Von Hagen set the standard of play for all of the present day players. He could run down any shot, hit from either side, never tire and always find a way to win. Ron Lang was simply the best player to ever play beach volleyball, period. I think maybe your memory of these players was when they were in their mid-30s, and still winning, but way past their prime.

• 16th-seed Mike Bright and Mike O'Hara and 18th-seed Ernie Suwara and Mike Bright, under today's rules, would force most of today's stars to have day jobs. These three players could hit and block with anybody today but had better ball control. With all due respect to the great talent of Steve Obradovich, he and Gary Hooper would not have gotten a game from Bright and O'Hara on any beach at any time.

I've never felt the urge to write and comment on any article I've ever read before, but someone needs to defend the talent and ability of these great stars. I could go on about Rundle, Selznick, Menges, Lee and Matt Gage - maybe the most underrated player of all time - but I won't. Next time, just do your homework and treat the legends with the respect they deserve.

Randy Nile
West Hills, Calif.

PAST CHAMPIONS — MANHATTAN BEACH

YEAR	TEAMS	YEAR	TEAMS	YEAR	TEAMS
1960	Mike O'Hara & Mike Bright	1971	Bob Clem & Larry Rundle	1981	Jim Menges & Randy Stoklos
1961	Mike O'Hara & Mike Bright	1972	Buzz Swartz & Matt Gage	1982	Mike Dodd & Tim Hovland
1962	Mike O'Hara & Mike Bright	1973	Bob Jackson & Fred Zuelich	1983	Mike Dodd & Tim Hovland
1963	Mike O'Hara & Mike Bright	1974	Ron Von Hagen & Tom Chamales	1984	Mike Dodd & Tim Hovland
1964	Mike O'Hara & Mike Bright	1975	Greg Lee & Jim Menges	1985	Mike Dodd & Tim Hovland
1965	Ron Lang & Gene Selznick	1976	Steve Obradovich & Chris Marlowe	1986	Sinjin Smith & Randy Stoklos
1966	Ron Von Hagen & Ron Lang	1977	Chris Marlowe & Jim Menges	1987	Mike Dodd & Tim Hovland
1967	Ron Von Hagen & Ron Lang	1978	Greg Lee & Jim Menges	1988	Karch Kiraly & Ricci Luyties
1968	Larry Rundle & Henry Bergman	1979	Jim Menges & Sinjin Smith	1989	Sinjin Smith & Randy Stoklos
1969	Ron Von Hagen & John Vallely	1980	Karch Kiraly & Sinjin Smith	1990	Brent Frohoff & Karch Kiraly
1970	Ron Von Hagen & Henry Bergman				

Ⓥ The Greatest

Mike Bright & Mike O'Hara

There are a few rivalries that will never die. ● Muhammad Ali vs. Joe Frazier. ● Magic Johnson vs. Larry Bird. ● Dan Quayle vs. Murphy Brown. ● Dane Quale vse. spelinge beese. ● Add to this list Mike O'Hara vs. Gene Selznick. ● It's not surprising. For in the mid-50s, right at the time Selznick should have been sitting all alone atop the beach volleyball world, along came O'Hara to challenge his supremacy. ● Although the feud began in 1953, it didn't really take root until 1960 when O'Hara hooked up with a 21-year-old kid named Mike Bright to dominate the beach. It is this rivalry more than his and O'Hara's record five straight Manhattan Beach Opens (1960-64) that Bright remembers the best. ● "Mike (O'Hara) always played incredible against Selznick," Bright recalls. "And Gene and Ron were both such great players. I always loved those games." ● As for O'Hara and Selznick's personal rivalry... ● "If we played today, I would be much better because I can get over the net more, and Gene could never bump," O'Hara says. ● "I won tournaments before and after O'Hara," Selznick says. "If I played him right now I'd still beat him." ● Some say potatoe...

Sinjin Smith Randy Stokl

What can you say? Or is it what can't you say? 133 w... Sinjin, 114 wins for Randy, 113 wins together. More... and recognition than all the others combined. ● Simpl... beach volleyball is Smith-Stoklos the way hockey is G... hoops is Michael and golf is boring. But more importan... all the numbers is that it was Smith-Stoklos who lifted... volleyball from a Southern California pastime to a nat... respected professional sport. ● "Each of us—myse... Hagen, Menges—took the sport to a certain poi... they've carried it from there," said Gene Selznick. ●... you win 100-plus tournaments, career highlights t... blur. But when pressed, both always point to their s... as a team in what has increasingly become an ind... sport. ● "Someone might beat my personal mark—pr... Randy, maybe even Kent," Sinjin said. "But for some... win 100 tournaments together, that might never be do... definitely my greatest accomplishment." ● The future... while the duo's relationship with the AVP has... recently—euphemistically speaking—Sinjin says they... back once again next season to challenge Karch and K... supremacy. But the fact remains that when you've set... standards, the to-do list starts to lose import. ● "My b... were passing Menges and then Von Hagen," Smi... "Once that happened, nothing else really ma...

Mike O'Hara (with trophy) and Mike Bright. photo: Kev...

34

On the Winning Team

Mike O'Hara

If medals were given to Olympians who had perpetuated the Olympic spirit not only on the fields of play, but also in their work as administrators of the Olympic Games, the name of Mike O'Hara would be among the winners.

In 1964, O'Hara was a member of the U. S. volleyball team that competed in the Tokyo Games. He was a college All American in 1953 and 1954, on the gold-medal-winning U.S. Pan American team of 1959, captain of the silver-medal-winning Pan American team in 1963, and a member of the 1960 national team. Twice he was voted the Most Valuable Player in America by the U.S. Volleyball Association. In 1966, O'Hara was inducted into the Volleyball Hall of Fame.

After his playing career was over, O'Hara became involved in the business and operations of sports management. He has organized and administrated thousands of athletic events, been an owner of sports teams, and acted as a commissioner of sports leagues and a college conference. He has also administered his own business management consulting firm. As a television commentator, O'Hara has distinguished himself on the major national networks, internationally covering the sports of basketball, volleyball, and water polo. He has also served as co-chairman of the U.S. Olympic Committee for Southern California (1972-1978) and as a member of the board of directors of the U.S. Volleyball Association (1970-1971).

O'Hara joined the LAOOC staff in 1980 as executive director of sports. His duties included hiring the committee's sports commissioners and negotiating with representatives of potential Olympic venues.

In 1982, O'Hara became vice president of television and communications, which put him in charge of negotiating television rights with broadcast companies throughout the world. He is also responsible for administering relationships with over 200 broadcasters in 105 countries. He also was responsible for the negotiations with 20th Century-Fox to produce the official Olympic Film and the international television series, "Countdown to '84" of ProServ Television. O'Hara developed and still oversees the Olympic Orientation Workshops for the 1,400 members of the LAOOC's Citizens Advisory Commission, a group of volunteers who provide professional expertise to the committee.

Although 20 years separate his performance as one of the world's best volleyball players from his work today as a talented manager, Mike O'Hara remains one of the all-around Olympians.

Michael O'Hara, member of the 1964 U. S. Olympic volleyball team and Vice President, 1984 Olympic Organizing Committee.

·· Pro Basketball For Big D ··

There has long been a feeling among basketball people that there are more good basketball players around than there are places to play. This past season less than 10 rookies made the grade in the National Basketball Association. With this in mind and with the boom in professional sports over the past few years, several businessmen from New York and California decided to form a new league; thus, the American Basketball Association was born.

George Mikan, the first superstar in professional basketball, and an attorney, was elected commissioner. Under his direction, 11 teams are ready to start their 78-game schedule in October. They are divided into the Eastern Division with New York, Louisville, Minnesota, Indianapolis and Pittsburgh; and the Western Division with Houston, New Orleans, Denver, Anaheim, Oakland and Dallas.

The Dallas franchise was originally awarded to a group from California but later control shifted to Dallas investers. The executive committee of the Chaparrals includes David Bruton, chairman of the board; Lindsay Embrey, vice chairman of the board; R. S. Folsom, president; Graham R. E. Koch, secretary; Joseph Geary, treasurer, and Michael F. O'Hara, executive vice-president and general manager.

O'Hara is a native of Waco and until recently was vice president of Art Linkletter Enterprises, Inc. Best known for his achievements in the world of sports, Mike was nine times named as a first team All-American performer in volleyball.

Cliff Hagan, former All-American and All-Pro basketballer is the coach. During Hagan's college career at Kentucky, other than being named to the All-American team he established an NCAA rebounding record by hauling in 528 during his junior year.

Cliff ranks among the most prolific point-makers in the history of pro basketball and one of the game's most dynamic players. He ranks high among all players on the league scoring charts with 12,433 points in 672 games for an 18.5 mark.

Max Williams, operations manager for the Dallas team, will be remembered well by basketball fans as one of the most colorful players in the Southwest Conference. Max was a master ball handler -- one that drew fans to the fieldhouse.

Williams, second high scoring guard in SMU history, is a former three-time All-Southwest Conference player.

The Chaparral roster follows:

CARROLL HOOSER: 6' 7" Two-time All-Southwest Conference from SMU.

HARRY FLOURNOY; 6' 6" Holds rebound record at Texas Western.

BOB WILSON: 6' 8" Had a fine record at the University of Kansas.

Mike O'Hara

Max Williams

Cliff Hagan

CINCY POWELL: 6' 8" University of Portland. Averaged 21 points per game in 1965-66.

ART BECKER: 6' 8" Third team All-American. Led in scoring for Arizona State in 1963.

NOLAND RICHARDSON: 6' 2" Was responsible for starting Texas Western on the road to power in basketball.

MELVIN REED; 6' 6" Leading scorer at Wichita State, All-Missouri Valley.

RUBEN RUSSELL: 6' 3" North Texas State. Led Missouri Valley in scoring for two years. All-Missouri Valley two times.

ANDY STOGLIN: 6' 4" Texas Western. Two years as shooter for the original Harlem Globetrotters.

JOHN BEASLEY: 6' 9" Texas A&M. All-Southwest Conference two times.

BOB VERGA: 6'1" Duke. College coaches first team All-American. Sixth pick in the pro-coaches All-American. AP and UPI second teams All-American. Player of the year in Atlantic Coast Conference in 1967.

The Chaparrals hope to add to this nucleus to form a basketball power in the new ABA.

A tentative schedule for the Chaps includes 39 games designated as home contests; however, five of these "home" games will be played in Lubbock.

The Chaps will open the campaign on Oct. 16 in Dallas against Anaheim. Home games will be played in Dallas Memorial Auditorium. The remainder of the season shapes up like this.

Oct. 16, Anaheim; Oct. 22, Indiana; Oct. 23, at Houston; Oct. 27, at New Orleans; Oct. 28, Pittsburgh, Nov. 7, Oakland; Nov. 10, at Louisville; Nov. 11, at Indiana; Nov. 13, Indiana; Nov. 15, Anaheim; Nov. 17 Houston; Nov. 19, at Houston; Nov. 21, Louisville; Nov. 22, at Indiana; Nov. 24, at New York; Nov. 26, Anaheim; Nov. 28, at Minnesota; Nov. 29, at Louisville.

Dec. 1, at New York; Dec. 5, Minnesota; Dec. 8, Anaheim; Dec. 10 at New Orleans; Dec. 11, Indiana; Dec. 12, New Orleans; Dec. 14, Oakland at Lubbock; Dec. 19, New Orleans; Dec. 21, Louisville; Dec. 26, Pittsburgh, Dec. 28, at Indiana; Dec. 29, at Pittsburgh; Dec. 30, at Minnesota.

Jan. 1, New York; Jan. 2, Minnesota; Jan. 5, at Pittsburgh; Jan. 6, at Louisville; Jan. 7, New Orleans; Jan. 8, at New Orleans; Jan. 9, All-Star Game; Jan. 10, Pittsburgh; Jan. 12, Houston; Jan. 14, at Anaheim; Jan. 16, at Oakland; Jan. 18, Louisville; Jan. 19, Houston; Jan. 21, New York; Jan. 23, at New Orleans; Jan. 25, at New Orleans; Jan. 26, Houston; Jan. 27, Denver; Jan. 28, at Anaheim; Jan. 29, at Denver; Jan. 31, at New York.

Feb. 1, at Minnesota; Feb. 2, at Pittsburgh; Feb. 5, Anaheim; Feb. 6, at Oakland; Feb. 7, at Denver; Feb. 9, Minnesota at Lubbock; Feb. 12, Denver; Feb. 15, New Orleans; Feb. 16, Denver; Feb. 18, at Houston; Feb. 20, Oakland at Lubbock; Feb. 21, at Houston; Feb. 25, at Oakland; Feb. 27, at Anaheim; Feb. 29, at Houston.

March 3, at Anaheim; March 4, at Denver; March 5, Oakland; March 5, Houston at Lubbock; March 10, at Anaheim; March 11, at Denver; March 14, New Orleans at Lubbock; March 16, Denver; March 17, at Oakland; March 20, New York; March 21, Oakland; March 22, at Denver.

(left to right) President and Nancy Reagan receiving the Olympic mural at the White House from LAOOC Vice Presidents Bob Fitzpatrick and Michael O'Hara.

Michael O'Hara with (top row) world champion Jim Ryan (miler) and Bob Seagren (pole vault) and other ITA pro athletes at the Gallager's Restaurant press conference in New York City in 1972. Fifty track meets on three continents resulted in fifty world records broken or tied.

Sports Illustrated archives

Citius, Altius, Opulentius

And richer these ex-Olympians-and others-certainly will be if former volleyball All-America and demon promoter Mike O'Hara succeeds in turning his dream of a pro-track circuit into reality.

by Joe Jares

Mike O'Hara's athletic specialty used to be leaping high and spiking a volleyball nearly straight down at 100 mph or more, and some of the balls he buried in the California sand 10 years ago still haven't been dug up. He spiked hard enough and often enough to make the U.S. Olympic team in 1964, make All-America seven straight years and get elected to the Volleyball Hall of Fame. Today, 40 years old and still skinny as a javelin, he is the founder and controlling stockholder of the International Track Association (ITA), a new set of initials in the crowded world of professional sports. And in going from volleyball star to track-and-field czar he made some interesting stops along the way.

This latest pro-track venture-none before has cleared even the first hurdle in this country-was revealed last month in New York, although ITA headquarters are in Los Angeles. O'Hara made sure to have some big names on hand, including four world-record holders-Jim Ryun, mile, 880; Lee Evans, 400 meters; Pole Vaulter Bob Seagren; and Shotputter Randy Matson-plus Richmond Flowers, a former top college hurdler who now plays safety for the New York Giants. Australian Distance Runner Tony Benson also has signed up. Ex-Villanova Miler Marty Liquori, who was a color man for the ABC telecasts from Munich, will be the master of ceremonies at ITA meets while continuing to run as an amateur.

Later ITA announced more converts: Miler Tom Von Ruden, two-miler Gerry Lindgren, Sprinter Warren Edmonson, 1968 Olympic 100-meter champion Jim Hines (who has been cut by three pro football teams), Long Jumper Henry Hines (no relation) and-the ultimate test of Liquori's announcing skills-SprinterJean-Louis

Ravelomanantsoa from Madagascar. He is the biggest mouthful since UCLA had a high jumper named Nagalingam Ethirveerasingam.

The basic plan is this: ITA will stage from 32 to 48 meets, starting in the U.S. and Canada this spring at the tail end of the amateur indoor circuit and moving to Europe this summer. As now scheduled, the first pro meets will be March 23 in Albuquerque and March 24 in Los Angeles. One of the last of the season in the U.S. will be at Madison Square Garden on June 6. At each one there will be about 50 athletes competing in 12 events-60-yard dash, 440, 880, mile, two mile, 60-yard hurdles, pole vault, shotput, high jump, long jump and two women's dashes-plus "special events," perhaps a shotputters' dash or a match race between Elke Sommer and Raquel Welch. ITA will pay all travel expenses for its contract competitors and guarantee minimum prize money for each event of $500 for first, $250 for second, $100 for third, $50 for fourth.

Does a pro-track circuit have a prayer for survival? Villanova Coach Jim Elliott wished it well but was pessimistic. "It has two chances, slim and none," he said. "They are adventurous people trying to do the impossible," said USCs Vern Wolfe, who later talked with O'Hara and became a member of his advisory board. "We have a difficult time making amateur track go with a relatively low cost factor, so how can professional track pay athletes, the expense of renting a facility, the equipment and the officials?" asked UCLA Coach Jim Bush. Other observers say the same guys will win all the time and bore even the stopwatch-clutching track nuts who eat statistics for breakfast; or that the fans will be tired of indoor track by the time the pros get out of the blocks in March; or that only the top dogs will make money.

O'Hara, who on the surface at least seems perfectly sane, has sunk more than $100,000 of his own money into ITA and insists he expects to get it back with interest, despite the frightening fact that the average break-even point for a pro meet will be $40,000.

"We want to make track and field the primary sport in the world; it was there once," he said. "We want to make money for ourselves and for the athletes and do something for the sport, and I'd bet heavily that we'll do that."

O'Hara has good reason to believe in himself and ignore scoffers. In the past six years he has become a specialist in packaging professional sports; not just teams or games or matches or tournaments, mind you, but whole leagues. In 1967 he was in on the founding of the American Basketball Association as an initial planner and co-owner of the Kentucky Colonels; he sold his share of the Colonels to become a co-owner and general manager of the Dallas Chaparrals, and finally he bowed out of the league profitably. The ABA is in its sixth season. O'Hara was also a founder of the World Hockey Association. He and a partner paid $25,000 for the San Francisco franchise, then six months later sold it to a Quebec group for $215,000.

"We have good momentum," says O'Hara. "This is our chance to benefit from our dues-paying in professional sports. We've had a single and a triple and we hope this one will be a home run." (They should also hope for a few dandy track-and-field analogies so they can stop publicizing baseball.)

O'Hara has been working on the pro-track project secretly for more than two years. He first discussed it with beach-volleyball crony Rink Babka, who sounds more like a Slavic dessert than what he is, a behemoth discus thrower, silver medalist at Rome in 1960 and the first man to skim the discus farther than 200 feet. They tossed ideas back and forth, then O'Hara started his research, which was interrupted by the WHA launching and piles of work at his management-consultant firm in West Los Angeles. On another detour, O'Hara tried to interest Jack Kramer in helping him run a pro-tennis tour a year before Lamar Hunt started World Championship of Tennis, but Kramer was too busy to be interested. All the while O'Hara was quietly poking around in track and field and asking almost everyone he came in touch with to sign a standard business nondisclosure form.

He was so successful that when it came time to approach the athletes, they had never heard of him, his projects or his volleyball exploits. He went after Liquori to run for ITA, but Liquori, doing graduate work in broadcasting at the University of Florida, talked himself into the announcing job instead. Matson, who admitted not having much motivation since the

1968 Olympics, was impressed with O'Hara's "businesslike approach" and was sold at their first meeting. He will continue to work for the Texas A&M alumni association while putting the shot on weekends.

O'Hara carefully stayed away from the Olympic team members until after their events were finished. Because he was not ready to reveal his project, he could not whip out a complete or even partial list of meets already scheduled. He had, however, been in contact with 103 of the largest arenas in Western Europe and North America, and facts about these, the dates they could be available, promoters who had the experience to act as front men and myriad other data were all recorded in something called the PERT Chart-standing for Programming, Education, Review and Technique. There was a lot more hard business and groundwork than mystery in the chart that O'Hara—half the time sounding like a business—school professor, the other half like a football coach-called his game plan.

O'Hara had one other handy tool, his checkbook, and he was not at all loath to show that to prospective pros. Seagren had been trying to forge an acting career in Hollywood without much success-pole-vaulting appearances kept interrupting-and was sick of being jumped on by the AAU for appearing in ads. Ryun, struggling along with his allergies and frustrations, had only $200 in his checking account when he left Kansas for the Olympic Trials, and now his wife Ann is expecting their second child soon. "My first thought was, 'Where do I sign?' " says Ryun.

That has been the reaction of almost every U.S. athlete once O'Hara gets past the first part of his sales pitch. One of his few failures was Kipchoge Keino, the outstanding Kenyan runner whom he chased to Nairobi after the Olympics, and even that is not an assured failure. O'Hara arrived back in the U.S. with a tape recording of Keino that said, however vaguely, that he might be joining up early next year.

The enthusiasm carries over to ex-athletes like Babka, 36, who as one of the financial backers of ITA is dragging out his old spikes and fondling them. Since the discus is strictly an outdoor event, Babka never competed indoors, but the competitive aspects of the tour have him excited anyway.

"I wish it was 1965 or '66 or even '68," he said wistfully. "I'd take up the shot!"

Finding investors was a cinch, said O'Hara, but putting together the management team ("the best group ever assembled to start a sports venture") took all his selling ability, which is considerable. The first man he went after was ex-decathlon champion Rafer Johnson, now a telephone-company executive in Bakersfield, Calif. They met at a sports program for retarded children at UCLA and O'Hara broached his ideas soon after. From there it was "about a four-month tag match before Rafer finally decided the cause was just," says O'Hara.

Johnson is chairman of the advisory committee and now has a financial interest in ITA. Max Muhleman, who negotiated WHA's TV contracts, will head ITA properties. Morris Chalfen, founder of Holiday on Ice, knows the ins and outs of every arena on both sides of the Atlantic, according to O'Hara. Perhaps most important, since ITA wants its shows to be well-paced and full of pizzazz, he has enlisted four experts on running meets, Stanford Coach Payton Jordan, Bert Nelson, publisher of Track & Field News, Wolfe of USC and Jim Terrill of Amherst.

The majority of the meets will be held indoors, where the spectators can plainly see who elbows whom in the turns and who splintered three hurdles to win that first-place check. The four are working to get rid of the cluttered infield that plagues most track meets, making them sometimes look like the floor of the New York Stock Exchange just before the crash. The San Francisco Examiner Games, for example, are often worked-the term is used loosely-by about 70 officials, many of whom stick around long after their event is over. By using the kind of sophisticated electronic timing and measuring equipment that worked well in Munich, Jordan and Nelson think they can reduce the officials to six, including a starter. And the athletes warming up for upcoming events will be asked whenever possible to do so somewhere else, out of sight. After all, Renata Tebaldi doesn't come out on the Metropolitan Opera stage and warm up her tonsils during one of Joan Sutherland's arias, right?

The old three-ring-circus idea is out. With the possible exception of the two-mile, there will be only one event going on at a time. "We won't be like the Perm Relays with two hours of mile relays," said Liquori.

Jordan, Nelson and the athletes themselves have a load of other innovations in mind. ITA will offer the services of a fashion consultant for uniforms, but ii a Dr. Delano Meriwether wants to sprint in bathing suit and suspenders, that's all right, too (though ITA does reserve a veto over costumes, just in case). Hey, why not a light that would whiz around the track in world-record time during a race, similar to greyhound racing's artificial rabbit? Right on. Or a mark to appear on the scoreboard almost the instant the shot lands? Have it, too. Or a decathlon to be run two events per meet for five weekends, or a self-replacing crossbar for the pole vault? Hallelujah, brother! Nelson talks excitedly about a proposed series of traffic lights that will tell the athletes when to stop and go. A yellow light at the pole-vault pit and Seagren will get ready at the top of the runway, then start moving when the green blinks on. Should he attempt a vault at the time the red light appears, he would lose his turn.

If a television contract materializes—and O'Hara has had very few serious talks with the networks so far—the athletes are so anxious to please that they'll try just about anything once. Especially Seagren, who says he once made a series of 16-foot vaults while wearing a battery pack taped around his chest and a sky diver's camera-helmet.

The most important innovation of all, of course, is the money M.C. Liquori will be handing out after each event. O'Hara is confident the ITA will be able to emulate tennis and set up some sort of Grand Prix point system that will bring fat checks at season's end. Sponsors of meets will also boost the prize money. O'Hara says that ITA could find the financial backing to hold out for 10 years if necessary. There are many who believe it will have to, and there are many who fear ITA will irreparably damage amateur clubs and the Olympics.

"I'll be there to see it," says former San Jose State Coach Bud Winter, "but it will be a sad night for those of us who still believe in amateur sports."

Kansas Coach Bob Timmons, longtime friend and mentor of Jim Ryun, disagrees. "It's strange how you hear so many people say they are disturbed about the idea of pro track but think nothing of professionalism in other sports. This probably can be traced to the Olympic idea of amateurism and the fact that track more than any other sport has come to be associated with the Olympics. But I can see nothing wrong at all with pro track. The track man should have his chance for equal rewards."

Surprisingly, before stepping down as AAU president Jack Kelly was not frothing at the mouth over the impending loss of Olympic-caliber track stars.

"I would hope that if they showed financial stability, nothing would happen to compare with what happened between the United States Lawn Tennis Association and Lamar Hunt's group," said Kelly. "They've really been at it. I feel tennis has become a big-time sport because of the pro players. Therefore, the response and participation on an amateur level has increased tremendously."

"Maybe pro track can do the same thing for track that Lamar Hunt's group is doing for tennis. If they do show such success, I for one would like to work with them instead of fighting them."

As badly as he wants ITA to succeed, O'Hara has decided, for the time being at least, to avoid as much as possible competing with the amateurs, although he admits ITA will be a "minor irritant at first." This is the reason he scheduled his meets to begin after the amateur circuit; why he announced that ITA will not sign athletes away from colleges; and why he did not approach Ryun, Seagren and others until after their Olympic events.

Still, the hint of bitterness to come popped up in Munich. O'Hara, aided by Liquori, was outlining his plans at a luncheon sponsored by Track & Field News. At that time he already had signed Seagren and Matson. A man in the audience yelled out, "Let's keep track and field pure and forget about turning the sport into another Roller Derby!"

"You may think Roller Derby is a joke," shot back the new czar, "but a lot of people attend their competitions and many of those skaters make a lot of money."

"This is an idea whose time has come," said Bert Nelson, acting as peacemaker. "I think we should give it a chance."

If it is to have a chance, O'Hara will have to be a strong leader in his position of owner/czar. He needs some superlative miles from his biggest drawing card, Ryun, and, given Ryun's history of self-doubt, allergies and bad luck in the last couple of years, that might not be easy. Ex-Kansas mile star Wes Santee remembers well the kind of race ITA can't afford to have.

There was a barely promoted exhibition race in Lawrence, Kans. in August as a kind of tune-up for Ryun. He was running against George Young and Canada's Grant McLaren in a two-mile. The twilight race drew about 3,500 people at $1 apiece.

"If Ryun had put out," said Santee, "if he hadn't fooled around and quit competing after a couple of laps, he and the other two could have toured around the country and drawn crowds everywhere.... To succeed, professional track will have to have the big names, but it will also have to have competition in every race."

Just in case the pot of gold at the end of the races is not enough incentive for Ryun and the others, or an athlete disappoints for any reason, O'Hara has retained the right to replace anybody who does not run, jump, throw or behave up to "ITA standards," whatever they turn out to be. Underneath his winning salesman's manner, he seems tough enough to wield the ax.

O'Hara is a tenacious competitor who hates to lose in business even more than in paddle tennis at his beach club. Recently he was chatting with some of the current volleyball stars when the subject of a beach tournament came up. It seems that on a Sunday evening when it was getting dark, cold and foggy at Santa Cruz and the finalists were exhausted from a long weekend of diving and leaping in the sand, they agreed to flip a coin to decide the winner and then go home. O'Hara listened and became visibly disgusted. He obviously despised the idea that athletes would not keep playing until they cramped up into human beach balls. He walked away, saying, "That's a bad story. Please don't ever tell it again."

Los Angeles Times

He Plans to Turn Sport Into League of Nations

Volleyball: Eight countries competing in Mike O'Hara's effort to put spotlight on athletes in non-Olympic years.

April 26, 1990 | CHRIS BAKER, TIMES STAFF WRITER

Mike O'Hara, the sports promoter who helped develop the American Basketball Assn., the World Hockey Assn. and professional track, has a vision:

The United States is meeting the Soviet Union in the championship match of the World (Volleyball) League and the Forum is sold out. A billion people, watching on a worldwide TV network, see Scott Fortune hit the winning point for the U.S. team.

Hmm? Sounds as if O'Hara, a former UCLA volleyball star, got spiked in the head one too many times. But they laughed when O'Hara devised the three-point shot for the American Basketball Assn., the World Hockey Assn. began signing underaged players such as Wayne Gretzky and Pro-Track started paying runners.

The ABA, WHA and Pro-Track were each making money when O'Hara left, and he predicts that the World League,

which begins play Sunday at the Forum, will succeed.

"Of all the things I've been involved in, I've never seen a league that has started with the credibility, experience and capital that this league has," O'Hara said. "Usually you sweat out the first year."

But O'Hara isn't sweating.

Mike O'Hara

The World League has a $4-million budget, of which $3 million will be underwritten by corporate sponsors and $1 million by TV contracts.

"The NBA didn't start out this well," O'Hara said. "The NFL didn't start out this well. All those leagues started out real shaky, but people forget about their humble beginnings."

Is the world ready for the World League?

It makes sense from a business and marketing standpoint. Sports Channel, which will televise the U.S. matches, is a cable network hungry for quality programming. And volleyball, which all but disappears in non-Olympic years, needs the exposure.

Fortune, who hit the winning shot in the gold-medal match in the 1988 Olympics, predicts success for the World League.

"I think it will be really big, especially in America," Fortune said. "The world championships are big in a lot of countries, but Americans don't really follow volleyball until the Olympics."

O'Hara has experience promoting volleyball, having run the Team Cup volleyball league at the Forum since 1984. Team Cup matches average 2,000 fans with the finals drawing 5,000. O'Hara hopes to expand on the base of Southland volleyball fans.

CHAPTER 18

A Future Way that the International Sport of Volleyball Could Become Even More Relevant

There are three entities that enjoy the distinction of having become strong international forces for good, and they are the sports of Indoor and Beach Volleyball, the YMCA, and Rotary, International. By working together on a specific project, in addition to operating on their own, they can synergistically set and accomplish specific goals, one at a time, that they could not accomplish as individual entities.

VOLLEYBALL

The sport of Volleyball has quietly become the fastest growing sport in the world, with 220 National Governing Bodies (NGB's), in 220 different countries, moving strongly ahead with programs for young and old, male and female, healthy and handicapped. They compare favorably with the terrific sports of Basketball, with 216 NGB's, and Soccer, with 204 NGB's in the world.

The reason for this tremendous continual growth is due to the economical, inexpensive use of both real estate and equipment. Where Basketball requires extensive ground cover and equipment and real estate, and Soccer Football requires even more real estate, which must be continually "nourished and made safe" for play, the sport of Volleyball has a much smaller court size, can be outside on sand, dirt or grass, and can accommodate from four to twelve players of all different ages, and both sexes on the court. The fact that Volleyball can accommodate more players per square foot than any other sport in the world, is a huge and important reason to go initially to a country that would welcome this type of facility and test out the optimum way in which this approach could be utilized for that specific community. The only equipment needed is a ball, net and rope or tape to lay out a court. The small amount of real estate needed must be flat and safe for athletes without shoes or wearing tennis shoes.

The other vital reason that the sport of Volleyball would be ideal for this project is the safeness of the sport. The Volleyball net separates the combatants, so that with six athletes on a side, (or four or two), there are no elbows, shoulders or knees clashing with one another. That is why the initial introduction by American missionaries of Beach Volleyball to the world was such a total success. It became the ideal way to invite the town leaders, and later the whole community, to come and enjoy "working out", and then being in a perfect mood to relax and learn about a specific religion.

YMCA

The second entity in this concept is the Young Men's Christian Association (YMCA). It is also a worldwide organization, with 45 million members in 125 countries, that encourages health, fitness and family values as the cornerstones of their organization.

The YMCA motto is "TO BUILD STRONG KIDS, STRONG FAMILIES AND A STRONG COMMUNITY." The YMCA Collage, later to be named Springfield College, directed by one of their leading professor's, Doctor James Naismith, invented the sport of Basketball in 1891. Four years later he contacted one of his star graduate students, Doctor William Morgan, who was then managing the Holyoke, Massachusetts YMCA. He informed Morgan that he was receiving word from many YMCA's across America that the more senior athletes were complaining about the injuries and stress problems that the sport of Basketball was causing, and asked him to come up with a sport that was less physically strenuous and injury prone, but still offered terrific exercise for all ages and both sexes, which could also include the ability of playing together in the same game.

Several weeks later, as one of many experiments to meet those objectives, Morgan came up with the concept of taking the bladder of a basketball, and then elevated a badmitton net to a height of eight feet, with equal amounts of males and females of all ages playing on each side of the net, serving, passing, spiking and digging the ball and VOILA! A totally awesome and ideally suited sport was born—VOLLEYBALL!

The fact that these two sports have become America's only two contributions to the Olympic Games is an indication of the huge role that the YMCA's played in motivating the world to become more fit and living longer.

While Volleyball had to compete in the marketplace of sport in America with the more established sports of Baseball, Football and even Basketball, in the rest of the world the only major competition was Soccer Football. As American missionaries journeyed throughout the world, to put Christian principles into practice, and to build a healthy spirit, mind and body for all, they found the sport of Volleyball was a tremendous way to get to really know the local folks in towns and cities everywhere. First it was a lot easier to find a small level surface, either on dirt, sand or grass (about 10% the size of a Soccer field) and hang a fishing net or a nope between two trees or step ladders and PRESTO! athletes could serve, volley and spike a light rubber ball, (or even a heavy, large balloon, if necessary) back and forth across the net. Volleyball became a tremendous "get acquainted" sport, with the net separating the two team of competitors, while everyone would obtain a lot of healthy exercise.

As these missionaries saw the tremendous contribution of Volleyball to their "get acquainted and talk religion" exchanges, they sent for better nets, balls and boundary ropes, and brought in the ideal sand or dirt for their Volleyball courts.

Today, Indoor Volleyball and Beach Volleyball are two of the quickest sports to sell out their respective stadiums in every Olympic Games. This huge additional credibility has added greatly to the popularity of both sports all over the world.

ROTARY INTERNATIONAL

There are 33,000 Rotary Clubs in 200 different countries. This global network of 1.2 million business and professional leaders is a potent force for good deeds and accomplishments. In order to qualify to be a Rotarian, you must convince the club in your town that you are a leading business man or business woman in your specific occupation. There is only one person in each category - lawyer, doctor, fire chief, teacher, etc. that can be in each club.

The leader of each of the Rotary Clubs worldwide has been challenged, by the President of Rotary International, to generate new concepts that will enable their organization, both locally, in their state and country, and internationally, to identify and organize worthwhile local, national and international causes to help others. Formed in 1905, the Rotary motto is "SERVICE ABOVE SELF".

I've been a Rotarian for about 15 years in Santa Monica, California, and about seven years ago our 125 members were asked by Rotary, International to each contribute a hundred dollars a year for five years to combat Polio (Infantile Paralysis) around the world. I was one of the 105 club members who were able to join that crucial fight for the many young people around the world that desperately needed those inoculations. Today, less than 1,000 young boys and girls IN THE WORLD that still have Polio, and Rotary, International is helping search the jungles of Africa to find those few young people who still need our help.

I have also served several terms on the Board of Directors of the United States of America Volleyball Association (USAV) and on their behalf represented them on the USA Olympic Volleyball Team in 1964. After starting the sport at UCLA in 1953 and '54, most of the UCLA and USC volleyballers moved over and represented the Hollywood YMCA, winning nine of the next eleven national championships. Our first and second Hollywood YMCA teams competed in the 1964 Olympic Trials in NYC, and six of us represented America in that first Olympic Games for Indoor Volleyball. In the Atlanta 1996 Games, Beach Volleyball became an Olympic sport as well. I can assure you that both of these international organizations, the YMCA and Rotary, International, are first class and caring, and their members are extremely dedicated.

The building of inexpensive, but very usable outdoor Beach Volleyball courts, initially throughout the countries that need the most help, and then ultimately throughout the entire world, would do a lot for the future business leaders, teachers, firemen, etc., of their respective countries. Russia would also be terrific pioneer of this concept, since they are great sportsmen, love Volleyball, and they could be an excellent role model for the other Eastern European countries. The three dedicated philanthropic organizations mentioned above would be an unbeatable team, if they were to lead this pilgrimage.

BOYS AND GIRLS CLUBS OF AMERICA (Locations Worldwide) (BGCA)

The Boys & Girls Clubs of America is rated by the Chronicle of Philanthropy, as the fastest growing, number one youth organization in the USA.

The reason they are so effective is defined by their five key characteristics:

1. Dedicated Youth Facility: The Boys & Girls Club (BGC) is "The Positive Place for Kids"… designed solely for youth programs and activities, it is their place!

Open Daily: The Club is available everyday after school (M-F 2:30 to 8:30) and all day during the summer. Some sites are open before school as well.

2. Professional Staff: Every Club has full time, trained youth development Professionals, providing positive role models and mentors and supplemented by trained part time employees and volunteers.

3. Available/Affordable to All Youth: BCG Clubs reach out to kids who cannot afford, or lack access to, other community programs.

4. The BCG offers diversified programs that appeal to the young people's needs and interests in six core areas: Education and Career Development, Character and Leadership Development, Health & Life Skills, the Arts, Sports Fitness & Recreation, and Special Initiatives.

Their Mission is "to inspire and enable all young people,
5. especially those who need us most, to reach their full potential as productive, caring, responsible citizens."

I was extremely impressed with the time-tested methods and programs that BGC uses to insure that at-risk, predominately low-income youth develop personal assets, skills and attitudes that enable them to succeed in school, in their communities, at home, and in their future as adults.

We are currently working with one of their highly talented leaders, Aaron Young, who heads up six BGC clubs in Santa Monica, California. They currently have 4,000 registered club members. Their largest club has three terrific outdoor short court basketball setups, built on asphalt, upon which he would like to produce three volleyball courts. He would like to have them ready for league play this summer, after their basketball season is over, that would serve teams for different divisions between ages 7 to 18.

I brought in Sinjin Smith, (a respected contributor to my book) who represents the Federation Internationale de Volleyball (FIVB), responsible for all outdoor/beach Volleyball subjects worldwide, now including these volleyball courts.

Within two hours time, we had worked out a way to make Aaron's request happen, with the ability to convert the three full sized volleyball courts back to basketball each year during their playing season, with no additional cost or time problems (see photo of subject courts). The total cost is going to be $2,000, and the three Volleyball courts will be ready for play this summer.

Aaron has also mentioned to me that his organization has collaborated with both the Lions Clubs and Kiwanis, concerning international projects in the past, and has achieved productive results. I asked Aaron for a quote concerning why he leads BGC and this was his reply: "On a personal note, I can speak directly about the impact that the Boys & Girls Clubs of America makes on a person because I experienced it first hand. From the time I was sevens old, I came to this club after school and over the summer. I went on to graduate from high school, and then college. After college I worked in the world of finance, only to return to the Club to give back to where I first started my life journey. Several of my childhood friends are now Club staff, others are long-time supporters of the organization. Others drop by to catch up from time to time. We share a common bond about many of the great times that we had as kids at this terrific sports and learning facility."

Due to the writing of this book, and my World Championship Tournaments and Olympic Games background and experience, I have been invited and am flying into the city of Doha in the State of Qatar on May 8, 2011. This is the 11th year of a conference called "Enriching the Middle East's Economic Future" which is presented by the Foreign Ministry of the State of Qatar and the UCLA Center for Middle East Development. This invitation has been extended from the Emir of the State of Qatar, H.H. Sheikh Hamad Bin Khalifa Al-Thani. The subject my presentation will be "Enriching the Regional Economic Future through Sports."

Previous speakers include President William Jefferson Clinton, UN Secretary General Ban Ki-moon, former NATO Commander Wesley Clark, former French President Jacques

Chirac, and H.E. Amr Moussa, Secretary General of the Arab League, Queen Ranin Rania Al Abdullah of Jordan, and President Tarja Halonen of Finland.

Beside the fact that this is truly a great honor, I have always been wanting to know more about this exceptional part of the world, and the individuals that manage their country's incredible oil and gas resources. My college major, for the first two years, was geology, and only the great attraction of the Southern California business world caused me the veer in that direction in my pursuit of undergraduate and Masters degrees.

Our hosts are combining two conferences, which will yield 700 participants from 100 countries! This has grown into an internationally recognized forum for dignitaries, investors and scholars to discuss pressing global policy issues and to conduct private business.

In addition to speaking on the impact of sports on regional business, and the role of franchises in the regional economy, I will be discussing ways that the Olympic Games and world championships have impacted various countries, and helped solve some of the desire on behalf of young children from growing up indoors, glued to the computer games and television set, instead of playing sports out of doors, where they can grow strong and healthy, instead of fat and sickly. This is not a regional problem, it is a world problem, but it is extremely serious, and therefore it is vital that it be addressed.

The final topic that could be discussed is the tremendous benefit that the hosting of regional and international sports competitions can have on any country, and the best approach to capture such a prize.

I will leave you all with my favorite thought, given to me by television star Art Linkletter, my last boss over four decades ago, as I went out to start my own firm, "WHAT IS IMPORTANT IN LIFE IS NOT HOW MANY TIMES YOU BREATHE, BUT HOW MANY TIMES YOU ARE LEFT BREATHLESS!"

L to R Aaron Young, President, CEO of Boys and Girls Clubs of Santa Monica, Michael O'Hara, President of O'Hara Enterprises International Inc.,Sinjin Smith Commissioner of Beach Volleyball Courts, Federation Internationale de Volleyball (FIVB), Brandon la Brie, Main Branch Director, Boys and Girls Clubs of Santa Monica.

Author's Biography

After playing college basketball at Santa Monica College, I matriculated to U.C.L.A. and joined the Delta Tau Delta fraternity, which happened to have a first rate volleyball court in the backyard, and a great number of players and spectators.

I quickly determined that my basketball skills would translate quickly for me, and that I enjoyed the daily competition even more, as we went on to win our school intramural competition. That allowed us to represent our school against USC, Pepperdine and Loyola, where we also found success.

My terrific setter, Rolf Engen and I went to UCLA Athletic Director Wilber Johns, with trophies in hand, and asked if we could represent the school at a forthcoming National Collegiate Championship at Boy's Town, Omaha, Nebraska. His response was affirmative, if we could spend our own funds, since there wan no budget for the school to use. We assured him that we would fund ourselves, and he loaned use some old basketball jerseys, and wished us great luck!

We returned ten days later, and presented him with a huge trophy, which we had to rope on the top of our car with six happy athletes crammed inside. When we suggested that volleyball might be a very successful sport to add to his roster, he thought a minute and responded, "I'm in the business of winning National Championships, and you'll have your varsity team next season." We repeated our successful run in Tucson the following year. In the following years, UCLA was the first university to win 100 National Championships, aided by our first two, plus seventeen more in the following years. (Note: I have since been fortunate enough to be inducted into the 200 strong UCLA Hall of Fame for all sports).

Left to right: Don McMahon, Hollywood actress Greta Thieson, Michael O'Hara

I was hooked on the sport of volleyball, and joined the Hollywood YMCA team, which was made up of mostly USC and UCLA players, and we were successful in winning National

Stockton, California's best spiker, number 2 on the left, was Chuck Nelson. In 1964 he moved to Los Angeles to obtain his CPA certificate at UCLA Graduate School. He became the CPA and CFO for O'Hara Enterprises International, Inc. We both make the Tokyo Olympics in 1964 and maintained our work and friendship relationships for forty-five years, and counting.

Open Championships in nine of the next eleven years. Along the way, we became the backbone of our national team, winning a Gold Medal in Chicago in 1959, and a Silver Medal in

Brazil, in 1963. In 1964, our Olympic host city, Tokyo, worked hard to add volleyball to their Games, and won the women's Gold medal, and the men's Silver, with the Socialist countries, led by Russia, winning the rest.

Meanwhile, Manhattan Beach became the "Wimbledon" of Beach Volleyball, by having the city far more strongly involved, including the placement of plaques of the winners on their major pier. My partner and I had the good fortune of winning the first five of those Championships, a feat that has never since been matched. Your author is proud to be inducted into the Indoor and Beach Volleyball Hall of Fame, in Holyoke, Massachuetts, where volleyball was born.

Mike O'Hara (No. 4) spiking, Jake Highland (No. 5) at Yokahama Stadium.

KERRY J.W. KLOSTERMANN
Secretary General

March 29, 2010

TO WHOM IT MAY CONCERN:

On behalf of USA Volleyball, I highly recommend the publication of Mr. Michael O'Hara's *"A Basic Guide to Volleyball"*. The book is not only highly informative, written from a true "insiders" perspective, but also entertaining and should appeal to the general sports enthusiast as well as volleyball's broad base of players, coaches, officials and fans.

Due to the unprecedented success of our teams in Beijing, volleyball and beach volleyball were featured in 11 of NBC's 16 prime time broadcasts of the 2008 Olympic Summer Games. Volleyball is the third most popular sport for high school girls behind only basketball and outdoor track and field. As of the 2006 / 2007 academic year there were 1,007 NCAA Women's volleyball teams, second only to basketball's 1,050. All of this coupled with USA Volleyball's 251,000 registered members and our intent to utilize our communication vehicles (website, e-newsletter) to promote this compendium of our sport suggests a viable market for this type of publication.

Sincerely,

Kerry JW Klosterman

Kerry J.W. Klostermann

USA VOLLEYBALL

Author Acknowledgements

The author would like to acknowledge the tremendous contributions of some of the most talented people in the sport of volleyball. No one has more expertise on the subject of rules then the late Dr. James Coleman, innovator and Rules of the Game Commission member for both the Federation Internationale de Volleyball (FIVB), and USA Volleyball (USAV) The same thing applies to USAV Director of Membership Development and Disabled Programs, John Kessel, concerning youth and high school volleyball and guidelines for parents, referees, volunteers, and fans, and game growth.

Sinjin Smith has the second most wins of any beach volleyball player worldwide. He is currently President of the FIVB Volleyball Council. Sinjin also does expert television commentating for the Association of Volleyball Professionals (AVP) for his Beach Volleyball sport. Doug Beal has been part of the USAV Men's National Team Program for most of his adult life, first as a player, then as a three time Olympic coach, including the winning of the 1984 Gold medal. Doug is currently leading our USAV organization as Chief Executive Officer and I give him great thanks. Dr. Gary Sato was a world class indoor volleyball player and assistant 1988 Olympic men's team coach, and has devoted his life to the sport. Gary, a practicing chiropractor, has returned to assist the USA National men's team through 2012, and is an expert on training methods and strategy. Jonathan Reeser, MD.-Ph.D is the past chair of the USA Volleyball Sports Medicine and Performance Commission, and a former member of the Medical Commission of the Federation Internationale de Volleyball (the International Federation governing the sports of Indoor Volleyball and beach volleyball world-wide). He currently serves as a team physician for the USA National Volleyball Teams. He works at the Marshfield Clinic Research Foundation, and resides in Marshfield, Wisconsin with his wife and two sons.

Jim McGinn, author of many theatrical plays and television dramas, has been a major asset concerning the way this book on the sport of volleyball stayed condensed and succinct. My sincere appreciation also goes to the finest of volleyball photographers, Artie Couvillon, thank you Artie. Many thanks to Greg Patterson, General Manager of the Santa Monica Beach Club, and his talented beach volleyballers, like Jack Powers, Paul Johnson and Les Meisenheimer, for supplying many wonderful vintage beach volleyball photos. Likewise, the Honolulu Outrigger Canoe Club, initial bastion for Beach Volleyball, led by the Haine family for many decades (Tommy, Marilyn, and Mark) provided facts, terrific photos and support concerning the accuracy of this book. Note that all photos, unless otherwise credited, are from my personal collection of volleyball pictures. Many thanks to my fabulous daughter-in-law, Victoria O'Hara, who has tremendously creative ideas about many subjects, and I love having her by my side. The same is true of my uniquely talented designer, Robert Aulicino, who had this publication standing tall, and very quickly, too.

Finally, my Olympic television associate, Clarence Chang, has secured the interest and support of a fellow Hong Kong University business professor. They have agreed to collaborate to convert this book into Mandarin so that another one-fifth of the world's population can learn more about one of the three most popular sports in the world!

My final thank you goes to my wife, Arlen, who put up with four long years of priority time, just because she know the love that I had for the sport of volleyball.

This book was made possible by their willingness to give of themselves for our sport.

I have just returned from the annual induction ceremony for

athletes and coaches, at the birthplace and Hall of Fame for the sport of Volleyball, Holyoke, Massachusetts. World renown athletes and coaches from five different countries came and were welcomed to this unique celebration. As the second inductee to this Hall of Fame, and a current member of the Nominating Committee, it was very exciting to have such a tremendous group of international star players and coaches to select from. Having the opportunity to meet or renew acquaintances with them was an even greater pleasure.

Indoor Volleyball athletes such as Gabriela Perez del Solar (currently a Peruvian Congresswoman), Aleksandr Savin of Russia, and Brazilian Beach Volleyballers champions Adriana Behar and Shelda Bede expressed great interest in having a translation of this book into their country's language, to assist in spreading the tremendous growth pattern of volleyball in their country. Celebrated championship Polish Coach Miroslav Pezedpelski expressed the same strong interest in this book, even though volleyball is the number one sport in Poland!